1993

Revolution and Romanticism, 1789-1834
A series of facsimile reprints chosen and introduced by
Jonathan Wordsworth
University Lecturer in Romantic Studies at Oxford

Cannning and Frere
Poetry of the Anti-jacobin 1799

George Canning and
John Hookham Frere

Poetry of the
Anti-jacobin
1799

Woodstock Books
Oxford and New York
1991

This edition first published 1991 by
Woodstock Books
Spelsbury House, Spelsbury, Oxford OX7 3JR
and
Woodstock Books
Wordsworth Trust America
Department of English, City College
Convent Ave and 138th St, New York, N.Y. 10031

New matter copyright © Woodstock Books 1991

British Library Cataloguing in Publication Data
Canning, George *b.1770*
    Poetry of the anti-Jacobin 1799. – (Revolution and
    romanticism, 1789-1834)
    I. Title   II. Frere, John Hookham, *b.1769*   III. Series
    821.709
    ISBN 1854770675

Printed and bound in Great Britain by
Smith Settle
Otley, West Yorkshire LS21 3JP

Introduction

A subterraneous Vault in the Abbey of Quedlinburgh . . .
Toads, and other loathesome Reptiles are seen traversing the
remoter parts of the Stage – Rogero appears, in chains, in a
Suit of rusty Armour . . .

Rog. Eleven years! it is now eleven years since I was first
    immured in this living sepulchre – the cruelty of a
    Minister – the perfidy of a Monk . . . Hah! the
    twenty-eighth of August! How does the recollection of it
    vibrate on my heart! It was on this day that I took my
    last leave of Matilda . . . I stood gazing on the hated
    vehicle which was conveying her away for ever. – The
    tears were petrified under my eyelids. – My heart was
    crystalized with agony . . .

The writer at this stage in *The rovers* – spoof German
tragedy, published in the *Anti-jacobin*, June 1798 – is
probably John Hookham Frere (schoolfriend of
Canning and fellow tory MP, working at the Foreign
Office). Rogero concludes his soliloquy, surprising the
reader with the words, 'Let me see whether the
damps of this dungeon have not yet injured my
guitar.' Parody becomes still more outrageous, as
Canning (aged twenty-seven, Under Secretary of State
for Foreign Affairs) takes up the pen:

[Rogero] begins the following Air with a full accompaniment
of Violins from the Orchestra:
    Whene'er with haggard eyes I view
      This dungeon that I'm rotting in,
  I think of those companions true
    Who studied with me at the U
      –niversity of Gottingen,
      –niversity of Gottingen.

[Weeps, and pulls out a blue kerchief, with which he wipes
his eyes; gazing tenderly at it, he proceeds.]

Sweet kerchief, check'd with heav'nly blue,
  Which once my love sat knotting in! —
Alas! Matilda *then* was true! –
  At least I thought so at the U
    –niversity of Gottingen,
    –niversity of Gottingen.

[At the repetition of this line Rogero clanks his Chains in cadence.]

It is all very light-hearted. The writers, it seems, share Wordsworth's view of 'sickly and frantic German tragedies' (Preface to *Lyrical ballads*, 1800), but are not going to be earnest about it. German extravagance of every kind is sent up: plot, character, emotion, language, even the incongruous use of stage-directions. As its name suggests, however, the *Anti-jacobin* is a political newspaper. Even in its lightest moods the satire has a purpose. *The rovers* is subtitled *The double arrangement*, drawing attention to Schiller's *Robbers* (translated 1792), but also to Goethe's newly translated *Stella*. Anarchy and misguided idealism are paired with sexual license. The *Anti-jacobin* is Burkean in its standards, attacking all that can be labelled radical or French, defending all that is decent and established within the fabric of English society. The paper appeared weekly during the parliamentary session, 18 November 1797-9 July 1798, coming to an end after thirty-six issues with the boast: 'the SPELL of *Jacobin invulnerability* is now broken'.

Canning was founder of the *Anti-jacobin*, but Pitt (Prime Minister since 1783) involved himself to a surprising extent, writing articles on finance, and a proportion of the leaders. Secrecy was maintained. Contributions were unsigned; copy was transcribed for the printer by an amanuensis so that handwriting should not be recognized. Frere had worked with Canning on the satirical *Microcosm* at Eton, and was a Foreign Office colleague. George Ellis, their main collaborator, was an older man, who had published *Specimens of early English poets* in 1790, and recently taken part in failed peace negotiations with the French. In July Canning had written to him in France: 'There is but one event, but that is an event for the world – Burke is dead.' William Gifford, chosen by Canning as editor, was author of the *Baviad* and *Maeviad* (1791 and '94), and later to edit the *Quarterly*. He was at once methodical and belligerent, setting the tone for the paper with his weekly refutations of the left-wing press (notably the *Morning chronicle*, *Post* and *Courier*), divided conveniently into LIES, MISREPRESENTATIONS and MISTAKES.

It was the satirical poetry that gave the *Anti-Jacobin* distinction, but some of the prose has a similar flair. Writing seems to have been a team effort. It was surely Canning and/or Frere who produced the brilliant account of a Meeting of the Friends of Freedom, billed on 30 November 1797 as 'an Authentic Copy of a part of a future *Morning chronicle*, which a Correspondent of ours has had the good fortune to anticipate'. *Mr Fox's birthday* (29 January 1798) has the same satirical edge, as does the best of the spoof correspondence. Letitia Sourby tells us on 18 December that her father, 'a respectable Manufacturer in the Calico line', has been seduced from his patriotic principles by 'hearing a Lecturer who went about the Country, reading History and Philosophy, and . . . "kindling a holy enthusiasm of Freedom"' (Thelwall, clearly). Miss Sourby's mother, meanwhile, has been 'sadly vexed' by her spouse's new 'French' attitudes to marriage:

It was but the other day that he told her, that if he were to choose again, by the New Law in the only Free Country in the world, he would prefer Concubinage – so he said in my hearing.

The satirical poetry of the *Anti-jacobin* begins as clever but limited parody, rising in the longer poems to a more imaginative, more general, evoking of the spirit of jacobinism. It is Southey who comes first under attack, travestied for his republicanism (*Inscription for the door of a cell in Newgate*), parodied in his use of classical metres, taunted with the stinginess of doctrinaire socialism. The true jacobin, we should recall, 'refrains from *relieving* the object of his compassionate observation . . . well knowing, that every diminution from the general mass of human misery, must proportionately diminish the force of his argument'. The *Widow* from Southey's *Poems* 1797 ('Cold was the night wind, drifting fast the snow fell') is scarcely more than an exercise in sapphics. It strikes a jacobin pose, however, and is duly overwhelmed by *The friend of humanity*:

> 'Tell me, Knife-grinder, how you came to grind knives?
> Did some rich man tyrannically use you?
> Was it the squire? or parson of the parish?
>   Or the attorney? . . .
>
> *I* give thee sixpence! I will see thee damn'd first –
> Wretch! whom no sense of wrongs can rouse to vengeance...'
>
> [*Kicks the Knife-grinder, overturns his wheel, and exit in a transport of Republican enthusiasm and universal philanthropy.*]

Southey is brilliantly, but rather too easily, despatched. The great achievement of the *Anti-Jacobin* poets is the creation of Mr Higgins, author not merely of

The rovers, but of *The progress of man* and *The loves of the triangles*. Higgins is the composite all-purpose jacobin poet, who writes to the editors 'from his study in St Mary Axe, the window of which looks upon the parish pump'. *The rovers*, he believes, will

do much to unhinge the present notions of men with regard to the obligations of Civil Society; and to substitute in lieu of sober contentment, and regular discharge of the duties incident to each man's particular situation, a wild desire of undefinable latitude and extravagance – an aspiration after shapeless somethings, that can neither be described, nor understood – a contemptuous disgust of all that *is*, and a persuasion that nothing is as it ought to be . . .

An earlier dig at Coleridge ('My good friend, the Bellman', too busy to supply a promised stanza of dactylics) confirms that St Mary Axe, with its bucolic pump, is his Devonshire birthplace, Ottery St Mary. On this occasion, however, the satire is mainly directed at Godwin. 'Disgust of all that *is*' had been expressed in *Caleb Williams* (1794), correctly titled *Things as they are*. In its portrayal of the 'shapeless somethings' that would guarantee a rational future, *Political justice* (reissued in 1796) was openly subversive of God and King and law.

Higgins's brilliantly funny *Progress of man* is dedicated to Richard Payne Knight as author of *The progress of civil society* (1796), a didactic poem in six books which does not at first sight look jacobin at all. Though writing in Pope's couplets, Knight is close to Thomson in his celebration of

Almighty Love! whose unresisted sway
Earth, air, and sea, with one accord, obey . . .

Book I of the *Progress* tells of Hunting, II of Pasturage, III of Agriculture, IV of Arts, Manufactures,

and Commerce, V of Climate and Soil; Book VI, Of
Government and Conquest, is more evidently
controversial. While deploring the excesses of the
Revolution, Knight sees the Terror as parallel to the
cruelties of the *ancien régime*. Britain he sees, not as
particularly vicious, but as waiting for revolution or
dictatorship –

> For come it will – the inevitable day,
> When Britain must corruption's forfeit pay,
> Beneath a despot's, or a rabble's sway.

Higgins's parody is presented in three fragments.
From the first there are hints that Knight's mild
liberalism is being crossed with the dangerous radical
views of Erasmus Darwin's *Loves of the plants*
(*Botanic garden*, part two, 1789):

ANIMATED BEINGS – Birds – Beasts – Fish – the Influence of
the Sexual Appetite – on Tigers – on Whales – on Crimpt
Cod – on Perch – on Shrimps – on Oysters. Various Stations
assigned to different Animals – Birds – Bears – Mackerel –
Bears remarkable for their fur – Mackerel cried on Sunday –
Birds do not graze – nor Fishes fly . . .

Canning's annotated copy of *Poetry of the Anti-
jacobin* claims sole authorship of *The progress*. He has
a marvellous ear, and the true humorist's sense of the
incongruous:

> First – to each living thing, whate'er its kind,
> Some lot, some part, some station is assign'd.
> The feather'd race with pinions skim the *air* –
> Not so the mackerel, and still less the bear . . .

The notes sustain, and develop, the humour, but
underneath it all there is the serious purpose. God's
'assigning' of lots, parts and stations, had been
questioned on many sides. Some even dared to ask

>   Whether the joys of earth, the hopes of heaven,
>   By Man to God, or God to Man, were given?

Canning's note at this point is important: 'See Godwin's *Enquirer*; Darwin's *Zoonomia*; Paine; Priestley, &c. &c. &c.; also all the French Encyclopedists.'

An immediate context for the *Anti-jacobin* emerges. *The enquirer* had come out in 1797, *Zoonomia* in 1794-7, Paine's *Age of reason* was 1795; Priestley had emigrated in '94 (leaving Coleridge to propagate his views in *Religious musings*, 1796). Godwin was an atheist, Paine a deist, Priestley a radical dissenter; the French Encyclopedists were guilty of asking the questions that led to the Revolution. Darwin was a still greater threat. His theory of evolution (often ascribed to his grandson) undermines the moral basis of society by denying the biblical account of Creation and the God-given pre-eminence of man. In a note to *Loves of the plants* Darwin had talked of the evolution of man as taking place over 'millions of ages'. The sequel, *Economy of vegetation* (*Botanic garden*, part one, 1791), offered a version of the 'big bang'; *Zoonomia* was no less speculative.

Outlining his principles as he submits *The loves of the triangles* for publication, Higgins (in this case, Frere) refers enigmatically to '*the eternal and absolute Perfectibility of Man*'. Darwin saw man as the result of improvement, but not as perfectible; Godwin saw him as perfectible, but not in a sense that was eternal or absolute; Coleridge (with the aid of Hartley) did see the human mind as potentially eternal, capable of merging with the divine. Frere has devised an elegant jacobin mélange:

if, as is demonstrable, we have risen from a level with the *cabbages of the field* to our present comparatively intelligent and dignified state of existence, by the mere exertion of our own *energies*; we should, if these *energies* were not repressed and subdued by the operation of prejudice, and folly, by KING-CRAFT and PRIEST-CRAFT . . . in time raise Man from his present biped state, to a rank more worthy of his endowments and aspirations; to a rank in which he would be, as it were, *all* MIND . . .

'There is one mind, one omnipresent Mind / Omnific', Coleridge had written in *Religious musings*, and ''Tis the sublime of man . . . to know ourselves / Parts and proportions of one won'drous whole'.

There may be some justice in the claim to have broken the spell of jacobin invulnerability. Certainly the paper had a major impact. Darwin's reputation was lastingly injured (the fact that he was right didn't matter), Godwin's would decline steeply from now on, Southey would write no more radical poetry. Political events, meanwhile, made pro-French sympathies more and more difficult to sustain. The take-over by the Directory in Paris in September 1797 was followed by the invasion of republican Switzerland in March, the threatened invasion of England, and the rise of Napoleon. In April 1798 Coleridge's recantation, *France, an ode*, was published in the *Morning post*. Insofar as literary jacobinism had a future, it lay with the poet whom the *Anti-jacobin* nearly names, but doesn't quite:

> And ye five other wandering Bards, that move
> In sweet accord of harmony and love,
> Coleridge and Southey, Lloyd and Lambe and Co.
> Tune all your mystic harps . . . (*New morality*)

Someone on the staff must have known that Southey, Lloyd and Lamb, were all on bad terms with Coleridge. Just possibly they knew too that Coleridge and Co. (Wordsworth) would be wandering soon to Germany. They could not know that *Lyrical ballads* – to be published in September – would establish Co. as the truly 'levelling muse'.

J W

POETRY

OF THE

ANTI-JACOBIN.

POETRY

OF THE

ANTI-JACOBIN.

———

LONDON :

PRINTED FOR J. WRIGHT,
PICCADILLY.

1799.

CONTENTS.

CONTENTS.

CONTENTS.

CONTENTS.

POETRY

OF THE

ANTI-JACOBIN.

No. I.

INTRODUCTION.

Nov. 20, 1797.

In our anxiety to provide for the amusement as well
as information of our Readers, we have not omitted to
make all the inquiries in our power for ascertaining
the means of procuring Poetical assistance. And it
would give us no small satisfaction to be able to re-
port, that we had succeeded, in this point, precisely
in the manner which would best have suited our own
taste and feelings, as well as those which we wish to
cultivate in our Readers.

But whether it be that good morals, and what we
should call good politics, are inconsistent with the spirit of true Poetry—whether " *the Muses still with free-*
" *dom found* " have an aversion to *regular* governments,
and require a frame and system of protection less complicated than king, lords, and commons;—

B

" Whether primordial *nonsense* springs to life
" In the wild war of *Democratic* strife,"
and there only—or for whatever other reason it may
be, whether physical, or moral, or philosophical (which
last is understood to mean something more than the
other two, though exactly *what*, it is difficult to say),
we have not been able to find one good and true poet,
of sound principles and sober practice, upon whom we
could rely for furnishing us with a handsome quantity
of sufficient and approved verse—such verse as our
Readers might be expected to get by heart, and to sing;
as the worthy philosopher MONGE describes the little
children of Sparta and Athens, singing the songs of Freedom, in expectation of the coming of *the Great Nation*.

In this difficulty, we have had no choice, but either
to provide no poetry at all,—a shabby expedient,—or
to go to the only market where it is to be had good
and ready made, that of the *Jacobins*—an expedient
full of danger, and not to be used but with the utmost
caution and delicacy.

To this latter expedient, however, after mature de-
liberation, we have determined to have recourse:—
qualifying it at the same time with such precautions,
as may conduce at once to the safety of our Readers'
principles, and to the improvement of our own poetry.

For this double purpose, we shall select from time
to time, from among those effusions of the *Jacobin*
Muse which happen to fall in our way, such pieces
as may serve to illustrate some one of the principles,
on which the poetical, as well as the political, doc-

trine of the NEW SCHOOL is established—prefacing each of them, for our Reader's sake, with a short disquisition on the particular tenet intended to be enforced or insinuated in the production before them—and accompanying it with an humble effort of our own, in imitation of the poem itself, and in further illustration of its principle.

By these means, though we cannot hope to catch " *the wood-notes wild*" of the Bards of Freedom, we may yet acquire, by dint of repeating after them, a more complete knowledge of the secret in which their greatness lies, than we could by mere prosaic admiration—and if we cannot become poets ourselves, we at least shall have collected the elements of a *Jacobin* Art of Poetry, for the use of those whose genius may be more capable of turning them to advantage.

It might not be unamusing to trace the springs and principles of this species of poetry, which are to be found, some in the exaggeration, and others in the direct inversion of the sentiments and passions, which have in all ages animated the breast of the favourite of the Muses, and distinguished him from the " vulgar " throng."

The poet in all ages has despised riches and grandeur.

The *Jacobin* poet improves this sentiment into a hatred of the rich and the great.

The poet of other times has been an enthusiast in the love of his native soil.

The *Jacobin* poet rejects all restriction in his feelings.

His love is enlarged and expanded so as to comprehend all human kind. The love of all human kind is without doubt a noble passion : it can hardly be necessary to mention, that its operation extends to *Freemen*, and them only, all over the world.

The old poet was a warrior, at least in imagination ; and sung the actions of the heroes of his country, in strains which " made Ambition Virtue," and which overwhelmed the horrors of war in its glory.

The *Jacobin* poet would have no objection to sing battles too—but *he* would take a distinction. The prowess of Buonaparte, indeed, he might chant in his loftiest strain of exultation. *There* we should find nothing but trophies, and triumphs, and branches of laurel and olive, phalanxes of Republicans shouting victory, satellites of despotism biting the ground, and geniusses of Liberty planting standards on mountaintops.

But let his own country triumph, or her Allies obtain an advantage ; straightway the "beauteous face of war" is changed ; the " pride, pomp, and circumstance" of victory are kept carefully out of sight—and we are presented with nothing but contusions and amputations, plundered peasants, and deserted looms. Our poet points the thunder of his blank verse at the head of the recruiting serjeant, or roars in dithyrambics against the lieutenants of pressgangs.

But it would be endless to chase the coy Muse of *Jacobinism* through all her characters. *Mille habet ornatus.* The *Mille decenter habet*, is perhaps more ques-

tionable. For in whatever disguise she appears, whether
of mirth or of melancholy, of piety or of tenderness,
under all disguises, like *Sir John Brute* in woman's
clothes, she is betrayed by her drunken swagger and
ruffian tone.

In the poem which we have selected for the edification of our Readers, and our own imitation, this day,
the principles which are meant to be inculcated speak
so plainly for themselves, that they need no previous
introduction.

INSCRIPTION

*For the Apartment in Chepstow Castle, where Henry Marten,
the Regicide, was imprisoned thirty years.*

FOR thirty years secluded from mankind
Here MARTEN linger'd. Often have these walls
Echoed his footsteps, as with even tread
He paced around his prison; not to him
Did Nature's fair varieties exist;
He never saw the sun's delightful beams
Save when through yon high bars he pour'd a sad
And broken splendour. Dost thou ask his crime?
He had REBELL'D AGAINST THE KING, AND SAT
IN JUDGMENT ON HIM; for his ardent mind
Shaped goodliest plans of happiness on earth,
And peace and liberty. Wild dreams! but such
As Plato loved; such as with holy zeal

Our Milton worshipp'd.   Blessed hopes! a while
From man withheld, even to the latter days
When Christ shall come, and all things be fulfill'd!

IMITATION.

INSCRIPTION

For the Door of the Cell in Newgate, where Mrs. Brownrigg,
the Prentice-cide, was confined previous to her Execution.

FOR one long term, or e'er her trial came,
Here BROWNRIGG linger'd.   Often have these cells
Echoed her blasphemies, as with shrill voice
She scream'd for fresh Geneva.   Not to her
Did the blithe fields of Tothill, or thy street,
St. Giles, its fair varieties expand;
Till at the last, in slow-drawn cart, she went
To execution.   Dost thou ask her crime?
SHE WHIPP'D TWO FEMALE PRENTICES TO DEATH,
AND HID THEM IN THE COAL-HOLE.   For her mind
Shaped strictest plans of discipline.   Sage schemes!
Such as Lycurgus taught, when at the shrine
Of the Orthyan goddess he bade flog
The little Spartans; such as erst chastised
Our Milton, when at college.   For this act
Did Brownrigg swing.   Harsh laws! But time shall
        come,
When France shall reign, and laws be all repeal'd!

No. II.

In the specimen of JACOBIN POETRY which we gave
in our last Number, was developed a principle, perhaps one of the most universally recognized in the Jacobin Creed; namely, " that the animadversion of
" *human laws* upon *human actions* is for the most part
" nothing but *gross oppression*; and that, in all cases of
" the administration of *criminal justice*, the truly be-
" nevolent mind will consider only the *severity of the*
" *punishment*, without any reference to the *malignity of*
" *the crime.*" This principle has of late years been
laboured with extraordinary industry, and brought
forward in a variety of shapes, for the edification of
the public. It has been inculcated in bulky quartos,
and illustrated in popular novels. It remained only
to fit it with a poetical dress, which had been attempted in the Inscription for Chepstow Castle, and which
(we flatter ourselves) was accomplished in that for
Mrs. Brownrigg's cell.

Another principle no less devoutly entertained, and
no less sedulously disseminated, is the *natural and eternal warfare of the* POOR *and the* RICH. In those orders
and gradations of society, which are the natural result
of the original difference of talents and of industry

among mankind, the Jacobin sees nothing but a gra-
duated scale of violence and cruelty. He considers
every rich man as an oppressor, and every person in a
lower situation as the victim of avarice, and the slave
of aristocratical insolence and contempt. These truths
he declares loudly, not to excite compassion, or to
soften the consciousness of superiority in the higher,
but for the purpose of aggravating discontent in the
inferior orders.

A human being, in the lowest state of penury and
distress, is a treasure to a reasoner of this cast.—He
contemplates, he examines, he turns him in every possible light, with a view of extracting from the variety
of his wretchedness new topics of invective against the
pride of property. He indeed (if he is a true Jacobin),
refrains from *relieving* the object of his compassionate
contemplation ; as well knowing, that every diminution from the general mass of human misery, must
proportionably diminish the force of his argument.

This principle is treated at large by many authors.
It is versified in sonnets and elegies without end. We
trace it particularly in a poem by the same author from
whom we borrowed our former illustration of the Jacobin doctrine of crimes and punishments. In this poem
the pathos of the matter is not a little relieved by the
absurdity of the metre. We shall not think it necessary to transcribe the whole of it, as our imitation does
not pretend to be so literal as in the last instance, but
merely aspires to convey some idea of the manner and
sentiment of the original. One stanza, however, we

must give, lest we should be suspected of painting from fancy, and not from life.

The learned reader will perceive that the metre is Sapphic, and affords a fine opportunity for his *scanning* and *proving*, if he has not forgotten them.

Cōld wăs thē nīght wīnd: drīftĭng fāst thĕ snōws
    fĕll,
Wīde wĕre thē dōwns, ānd shĕltĕrlēss ănd nākĕd:
Whēn ă poōr wānd'rĕr strŭgglĕd ōn hĕr joūrnĕy
         Weary̆ ănd wāy-sōre.

This is enough: unless the reader should wish to be informed how

Fāst o'ĕr thē blēak hēath rāttlĭng drōve ă chārĭŏt;

or how, not long after,

Loūd blĕw thē wīnd, ūnheărd wăs hēr cŏmplāinĭng—
         ōn wĕnt thĕ hōrsemān.

We proceed to give our imitation, which is of the *Amœbœan* or *Collocutory* kind.

IMITATION.

SAPPHICS.

The Friend of Humanity and the Knife Grinder.

FRIEND OF HUMANITY.

" Needy Knife-grinder! whither are you going?
Rough is the road, your wheel is out of order—
Bleak blows the blast;—your hat has got a hole in't,
So have your breeches!

" Weary Knife-grinder! little think the proud ones,
Who in their coaches roll along the turnpike-
-road, what hard work 'tis crying all day " Knives and
" Scissars to grind O!"

" Tell me, Knife-grinder, how you came to grind
knives?
Did some rich man tyrannically use you?
Was it the squire? or parson of the parish?
Or the attorney?

" Was it the squire, for killing of his game? or
Covetous parson, for his tithes distraining?
Or roguish lawyer, made you lose your little
All in a lawsuit?

"(Have you not read the Rights of Man, by Tom Paine?)
Drops of compassion tremble on my eyelids,
Ready to fall, as soon as you have told your
                    Pitiful story."

KNIFE-GRINDER.

" Story! God bless you! I have none to tell, sir,
Only last night a-drinking at the Chequers,
This poor old hat and breeches, as you see, were
                    Torn in a scuffle.

" Constables came up for to take me into
Custody; they took me before the justice;
Justice Oldmixon put me in the parish-
                    -Stocks for a vagrant.

" I should be glad to drink your Honour's health in
A pot of beer, if you will give me sixpence;
But for my part, I never love to meddle
                    With politics, sir."

FRIEND OF HUMANITY.

" *I* give thee sixpence! I will see thee damn'd first—
Wretch! whom no sense of wrongs can rouse to ven-
        geance—
Sordid, unfeeling, reprobate, degraded,
                    Spiritless outcast!"
[*Kicks the Knife-grinder, overturns his wheel, and exit in a
    transport of Republican enthusiasm and universal philan-
    thropy.*]

No. III.

Nov. 30.
*We have received the following from a Loyal Correspondent,
and we shall be very happy at any time to be relieved, by
communications of a similar tendency, from the drudgery
of Jacobinical imitations.*

―――――――

THE INVASION;

OR, THE BRITISH WAR SONG.

To the Tune of " Whilst happy in my native land."

I.

Whilst happy in our native land,
    So great, so famed in story,
Let's join, my friends, with heart and hand
    To guard our country's glory:
When Britain calls, her valiant sons
    Will rush in crowds to aid her—
Snatch, snatch your muskets, prime your guns,
    And crush the fierce invader!
        Whilst every Briton's song shall be,
        " O give us death—or victory!"

II.

Long had this favour'd isle enjoy'd
  True comforts, past expressing,
When *France* her hellish arts employ'd
  To rob us of each blessing:
These from our hearths by force to tear
  (Which long we've learn'd to cherish)
Our frantic foes shall vainly dare;
  We'll keep 'em, or we'll perish—
    And every day our song shall be,
    " O give us death—or victory!"

III.

Let France in savage accents sing
  Her bloody Revolution;
We prize our Country, love our King,
  Adore our Constitution;
For these we'll every danger face,
  And quit our rustic labours;
Our ploughs to firelocks shall give place,
  Our scythes be changed to sabres.
    And clad in arms, our song shall be,
    " O give us death—or victory!"

IV.

Soon shall the proud invaders learn,
  When bent on blood and plunder,
That British bosoms nobly burn
  To brave their cannon's thunder:

Low lie those heads, whose wily arts
  Have plann'd the world's undoing!
Our vengeful blades shall reach those hearts
  Which seek our country's ruin;
    And night and morn our song shall be,
    " O give us death—or victory!"

V.

When, with French blood our fields manured,
  The glorious struggle's ended,
We'll sing the dangers we've endured,
  The blessings we've defended;
O'er the full bowl our feats we'll tell,
  Each gallant deed reciting;
And weep o'er those who nobly fell
  Their country's battle fighting—
    And ever thence our song shall be,
    " 'Tis Valour leads to Victory."

No. IV.

Decemb. 4.

We have been favoured with the following specimen of Jacobin Poetry, which we give to the world without any comment or imitation. We are informed (we know not how truly) that it will be sung at the Meeting of the Friends of Freedom; an account of which is anticipated in our present Paper.

LA SAINTE GUILLOTINE.

A NEW SONG.

ATTEMPTED FROM THE FRENCH.

Tune, " O'er the vine-cover'd hills and gay regions of France."

I.

From the blood bedew'd vallies and mountains of
    France,
See the Genius of Gallic invasion advance!
Old ocean shall waft her, unruffled by storm,
While our shores are all lined with the *Friends of Reform.**

    * See Proclamation of the Directory.

Confiscation and Murder attend in her train,
With meek-eyed Sedition, the daughter of Paine ; *
While her sportive *Poissardes* with light footsteps are
    seen
To dance in a ring round the gay *Guillotine.*†

II.

To *London,* " the rich, the defenceless"‡ she comes—
Hark ! my boys, to the sound of the Jacobin drums !
See Corruption, Prescription, and Privilege fly,
Pierced through by the glance of her blood-darting eye.
While patriots, from prison and prejudice freed,
In soft accents shall lisp the Republican Creed,
And with tri-colour'd fillets, and cravats of green,
Shall crowd round the altar of *Saint Guillotine.*

III.

See the level of Freedom sweeps over the land—
The vile Aristocracy's doom is at hand !
Not a seat shall be left in a House *that we know,*
But for *Earl Buonaparte* and *Baron Moreau.*—
But the rights of the Commons shall still be respected,
Buonaparte himself shall approve the elected ;
And the Speaker shall march with majestical mien,
And make his three bows to the grave *Guillotine.*

* The "*too long calumniated* author of the Rights of Man."
—See a Sir Something Burdet's speech at the Shakspeare, as
referred to in the *Courier* of Nov. 30.
† The Guillotine at Arras was, as is well known to every
Jacobin, painted " *Couleur de Rose.*"
‡ See *Weekly Examiner,* No. II.   Extract from *the Courier.*

IV.

Two heads, says the proverb, are better than one,
But the Jacobin choice is for Five Heads or none.
By Directories only can Liberty thrive;
Then down with the ONE, Boys! and up with the FIVE!
How our bishops and judges will stare with amazement,
When their heads are thrust out at the *National Case-
ment!* *

When the *National Razor** has shaved them quite clean,
What a handsome oblation to *Saint Guillotine!*

* *La petite Fenêtre*, and *la Razoire Nationale*, fondling expressions applied to the Guillotine by the Jacobins in France,
and their pupils here.

C

No. V.

Decemb. 11.

W E have already hinted at the principle by which the followers of the Jacobinical Sect are restrained from the exercise of their own favourite virtue of Charity. The force of this prohibition, and the strictness with which it is observed, are strongly exemplified in the following poem. It is the production of the same Author, whose happy effort in English Sapphics we presumed to imitate; the present effusion is in Dactylics, and equally subject to the laws of Latin Prosody.

THE SOLDIER'S WIFE.

Wēary̆ wăy-wāndĕrĕr, lānguĭd ănd sīck ăt hĕart,
Trăvĕllĭng pāinfŭlly ōvĕr thĕ rūggĕd rŏad,
Wīld vĭsăg'd wāndĕrĕr—āh fŏr thy̆ hēavy̆ chănce.

We think that we see him fumbling in the pocket of his blue pantaloons; that the splendid shilling is about to make its appearance, and to glitter in the eyes, and glad the heart of the poor sufferer.—But no such thing —the Bard very calmly contemplates her situation, which he describes in a pair of very pathetical stanzas;

and after the following well-imagined topic of consolation, concludes by leaving her to Providence.

———

Thy husband will never return from the war again ;
Cold is thy hopeless heart, *even as Charity*,
Cold are thy famished babes—*God help thee*, widow'd
    one !

———

We conceived that it would be necessary to follow
up this general rule with the particular exception, and
to point out one of those cases in which the embargo
upon Jacobin Bounty is sometimes suspended : with
this view we have subjoined the poem of

THE SOLDIER'S FRIEND.

DACTYLICS.

COME, little Drummer Boy, lay down your knap_
    sack here :
I am the Soldier's Friend—here are some books for you ;
Nice clever books by Tom Paine, the philanthropist.

Here's half-a-crown for you—here are some handbills
    too—
Go to the Barracks, and give all the Soldiers some.
Tell them the Sailors are all in a Mutiny.
    [*Exit Drummer Boy, with Handbills, and Half-a-
    crown.—Manet Soldier's Friend.*

Liberty's friends thus all learn to amalgamate,
Freedom's volcanic explosion prepares itself,
Despots shall bow to the Fasces of Liberty,
   Reason, philosophy, " fiddledum diddledum,"
   Peace and Fraternity, higgledy, piggledy,
   Higgledy, piggledy, " fiddledum, diddledum."

                Et cætera, et cætera, et cætera.

SONNET. TO LIBERTY.

JUST Guardian of man's social bliss ! for thee
   The paths of danger gladly would I tread :
   For thee ! contented, join the glorious dead,
Who nobly scorn'd a life that was not free !

But worse than death it pains my soul, to see
   The Lord of Ruin, by wild Uproar led,
   Hell's first-born, ANARCHY, exalt his head,
And seize thy throne, and bid us bow the knee !

What though his iron sceptre, blood-imbrued,
   Crush half the nations with resistless might ;
Never shall this firm spirit be subdued :
   In chains, in exile, still the chanted rite,
O LIBERTY ! to thee shall be renew'd :
   O still be sea-girt ALBION thy delight !

                            D.

No. VI.

Decemb. 18.

W E cannot enough congratulate ourselves, on having been so fortunate as to fall upon the curious specimens of classical metre and correct sentiment, which we have made the subjects of our late Jacobinical Imitations.

The fashion of admiring and imitating these productions has spread in a surprising degree. Even those who sympathize with the principles of the writer selected as our model, seem to have been struck with the ridicule of his poetry.

There appeared in the *Morning Chronicle* of Monday a *Sapphic Ode*, apparently written by a friend and associate of our Author, in which he is however travestied most unmercifully. And to make the joke the more pointed, the learned and judicious Editor contrived to print the ode *en masse*, without any order of lines, or division of stanza; so that it was not discovered to be *verse* till the next day, when it was explained in a hobbling *erratum*.

We hardly know which to consider as the greater object of compassion in this case—the original *Odist* thus parodied by his friend, or the mortified *Parodist* thus mutilated by his Printer. " *Et tu Brute!*" has probably been echoed from each of these worthies to his murderer, in a tone that might melt the hardest heart to pity.

We cordially wish them joy of each other, and we resign the modern *Lesbian lyre* into their hands without envy or repining.

Our Author's DACTYLICS have produced a second imitation (conveyed to us from an unknown hand), with which we take our leave of this species of poetry also.

THE SOLDIER'S WIFE.

DACTYLICS.

" Wēarȳ wăy-wāndĕrĕr, &c. &c.

IMITATION.

DACTYLICS.

Being the quintessence of all the Dactylics that ever were, or ever will be written.

HUMBLY ADDRESSED TO THE AUTHOR OF THE ABOVE.

WEARISOME Sonnetteer, feeble and querulous,
Painfully dragging out thy demo-cratic lays—
Moon-stricken Sonnetteer, "ah! for thy heavy chance!"

Sorely thy Dactylics lag on uneven feet:
Slow is the syllable which thou would'st urge to speed,
Lame and o'erburthen'd, and " screaming its wretch-
    " edness!"

†   *   *   *   *   *   *   *   *   *   *   *

Ne'er talk of ears again! look at thy spelling-book;
Dilworth and *Dyche* are both mad at thy quantities—
DACTYLICS, call'st thou 'em?—" God help thee, silly
    " one!"

———————

The Verses, which we here present to the Public, were writ-
ten immediately after the Revolution of the Fourth of Sep-
tember. We should be much obliged to any of our Classical
and Loyal Correspondents, for an English Translation of
them.

IPSA mali Hortatrix scelerumque uberrima Mater
In se prima suos vertit lymphata furores,
Luctaturque diù secum, et conatibus ægris
Fessa cadit, proprioque jacet labefacta veneno.

† My worthy friend, the Bellman, had promised to supply an additional stanza; but the business of assisting the
Lamplighter, Chimney sweeper, &c. with Complimentary
Verses for their worthy Masters and Mistresses, pressing on
him at this season, he was obliged to decline it.

Mox tamen ipsius rursúm violentia morbi
Erigit ardentem furiis, ultróque minantem
Spargere bella procul, vastæque incendia cladis,
Civilesque agitare faces, totumque per orbem
Sceptra super Regum et Populorum subdita colla
Ferre pedem, et sanctas Regnorum evertere sedes.

Aspicis! Ipsa sui bacchatur sanguine Regis,
Barbaraque ostentans feralis signa triumphi,
Mole giganteâ campis prorumpit apertis,
Successu scelerum, atque insanis viribus audax.

At quâ Pestis atrox rapido se turbine vertit,
Cernis ibi, priscâ morum compage solutâ,
Procubuisse solo civilis fœdera vitæ,
Et quodcunque Fides, quodcunque habet alma verendi
Religio, Pietasque et Legum fræna sacrarum.

Nec spes Pacis adhúc—necdum exsaturata rapinis
Effera Bellatrix, fusove expleta cruore.
Crescit inextinctus Furor, atque exæstuat ingens
Ambitio, immanisque irâ Vindicta renatâ
Relliquias Soliorum et adhuc restantia Regna
Flagitat excidio, prædæque incumbit opimæ.

Una etenim in mediis Gens intemerata ruinis
Libertate probâ, et justo libramine rerum,
Securum faustis degit sub legibus ævum;
Antiquosque colit mores, et jura Parentum
Ordine firma suo, sanoque intacta vigore,

Servat adhuc, hominumque fidem, curamque Deorum.
Eheu! quanta odiis avidoque alimenta furori!
Quanta profanatas inter spoliabitur aras
Victima! si quando versis Victoria fatis
Annuerit scelus extremum, terrâque subactâ
Impius Oceani sceptrum fædaverit Hostis!

147, 109

No. VII.

Dec. 25.

We have been favoured with a Translation of the Latin
Verses inserted in our last Number. We have little doubt
that our Readers will agree with us, in hoping that this
may not be the last contribution which we shall receive
from the same hand.

PARENT of countless crimes, in headlong rage,
War with herself see frantic *Gallia* wage,
'Till worn and wasted by intestine strife,
She falls—her languid pulse scarce quick with life.
But soon she feels thro' every trembling vein,
New strength collected from convulsive pain :
Onward she moves, and sounds the dire alarm,
And bids insulted nations haste to arm ;
Spreads wide the waste of War, and hurls the brand
Of Civil Discord o'er each troubled land,
While Desolation marks her furious course,
And thrones subverted bow beneath her force.

Behold! she pours her Monarch's guiltless blood,
And quaffs with savage joy the crimson flood ;
Then, proud the deadly trophies to display
Of her foul crime, resistless bursts away,

Unaw'd by justice, unappall'd by fear,
And runs with giant strength her mad career.

Where'er her banners float in barbarous pride,
Where'er her conquest rolls its sanguine tide,
There, the fair fabric of establish'd law,
There social order, and religious awe,
Sink in the general wreck ; indignant there
Honour and Virtue fly the tainted air ;
Fly the mild duties of domestic life
That cheer the parent, that endear the wife,
The lingering pangs of kindred grief assuage,
Or soothe the sorrows of declining age.—

Nor yet can Hope presage th' auspicious hour,
When Peace shall check the rage of lawless Power ;
Nor yet th' insatiate thirst of blood is o'er,
Nor yet has Rapine ravaged every shore.
Exhaustless Passion feeds th' augmented flame,
And wild Ambition mocks the voice of Shame :
Revenge, with haggard look and scowling eyes,
Surveys with horrid joy th' expected prize ;
Broods o'er each remnant of monarchic sway,
And dooms to certain death his fancied prey.—

For midst the ruins of each falling state,
ONE FAVOUR'D NATION braves the general fate,
One favour'd nation, whose impartial laws
Of sober Freedom vindicate the cause ;

Her simple manners, midst surrounding crimes,
Proclaim the genuine worth of ancient times ;
True to herself, unconquerably bold,
The Rights her valour gain'd she dares uphold ;
Still with pure faith her promise dares fulfil,
Still bows submission to th' Almighty Will.—

Just Heav'n ! how Envy kindles at the sight !
How mad Ambition plans the desperate fight !
With what new fury Vengeance hastes to pour
Her tribes of rapine from yon crowded shore !
Just Heav'n ! how fair a victim at the shrine
Of injur'd Freedom shall her life resign,
If e'er, propitious to the vows of hate,
Unsteady Conquest stamp our mournful fate,
If e'er proud France usurp our ancient reign,
And ride triumphant o'er the insulted main !

*   *   *   *   *   *   *

Far hence the unmanly thought—The voice of Fame
Wafts o'er the applauding deep her Duncan's name.
What tho' the Conqueror of th' Italian plains
Deem nothing gain'd, while this fair Isle remains,
Tho' his young breast with rash presumption glow,
He braves the vengeance of no vulgar foe :
Conqueror no more, full soon his laurel'd pride
Shall perish—whelm'd in Ocean's angry tide ;
His broken bands shall rue the fatal day,
And scatter'd fleets proclaim BRITANNIA's sway.

No. VIII.

Jan. 1st, 1798.

A Correspondent has adapted the beautiful poem of the Battle of Sabla, in " Carlyle's Specimens of Arabian Poetry," to the circumstances of the present moment. We shall always be happy to see the poetry of other times and nations so successfully engaged in the service of our Country, and of the present order of Society.

THE CHOICE.

(FROM THE BATTLE OF SABLA, IN CARLYLE'S SPECIMENS OF ARABIAN POETRY.)

I.

Hast thou not seen th' insulting foe
   In fancied triumphs crown'd?
And heard their frantic rulers throw
   These empty threats around?
" Make now YOUR CHOICE! The terms we give,
   " Desponding Britons, hear!
" These fetters on your hands receive,
   " Or in your hearts the spear."

Can we forget our old renown;
   Resign the empire of the sea;
And yield at once our Sovereign's crown,
   Our ancient Laws and Liberty?

Shall thus the fierce Destroyer's hand
Pass unresisted o'er our Native Land ?
Our Country sink, to barb'rous force a prey,
And *ransom'd* England bow to *Gallic* sway ?

II.

" Is then the contest o'er ?" we cried,
  " And lie we at your feet ?
" And dare you vauntingly decide
  " The fortune we shall meet ?
" A brighter day we soon shall see ;
  " No more the prospect lours ;
" And Conquest, Peace, and Liberty,
  " Shall gild our future hours."

Yes ! we will guard our old renown ;
  Assert our empire of the sea ;
And keep untouch'd our Sovereign's crown,
  Our ancient Laws and Liberty.

Not thus the fierce Destroyer's hand
Shall scatter ruin o'er this smiling land ;
No barb'rous force shall here divide its prey ;
Nor *ransom'd* England bow to *Gallic* sway.

III.

The Foe advance. In firm array
  We'll rush o'er Albion's sands—
Till the red sabre marks our way
  Amid their yielding bands !

Then, as they lie in death's cold grasp,
   We'll cry, " OUR CHOICE IS MADE !
" These hands the sabre's hilt shall clasp,
   " Your hearts shall feel the blade."

Thus Britons guard their ancient fame,
   Assert their empire o'er the sea,
And to the envying world proclaim,
   One Nation still is brave and free—

Resolv'd to conquer or to die,
True to their KING, their LAWS, their LIBERTY :
No barb'rous foe here finds an easy prey—
Un-ransom'd England spurns all foreign sway.

———————

The following poem has been transmitted to us, without pre-
face or introduction, by a gentleman of the name of Ireland. *We apprehend from the peculiarities of the style,*
that it must be the production of a remote period. We are
likewise inclined to imagine, that it may contain allusions
to some former event in English history. What that event
may have been, we must submit to the better judgment and
superior information of our Readers ; from whom we im-
patiently expect a solution of this interesting question. The
Editor has been influenced solely by a sense of its poetical
merit.

THE DUKE AND THE TAXING-MAN.

Whilome there liv'd in fair Englonde
    A Duke of peerless wealth,
And mickle care he took of her
    Old Constitution's health.

Full fifty thousand pounds and more
    To him his vassals paid,
But ne to King, ne Countree, he
    Would yield th' assessment made.

The taxing-man, with grim viságe
    Came pricking on the way,
The taxing-man, with wrothful words,
    Thus to the Duke did say:

" Lord Duke, Lord Duke, thou'st hid from me,
    " As sure as I'm alive,
" Of goodly palfreys *seventeen*,
    " Of varlets *twenty-five*."

Then out he drew his gray goose quill,
    Ydipp'd in ink so black,
And sorely to surcharge the Duke,
    I trowe, he was ne slack.

Then 'gan the Duke to looken pale,
   And stared as astound,
* Twaie coneynge Clerks, eftsoons he spies
   Sitting their board around.

" O woe is me," then cried the Duke,
   " Ne mortal wight but errs!
" I'll hie to yon twaie coneynge Clerks,
   "Yclept Commissioners."

The Duke he hied him to the board,
   And straught 'gan for to say,
" † A seely wight I am, God wot,
   " Ne ken I the right way.

" These varlets twenty-five were ne'er
   " *Liveried in white and red*,
" Withouten this, what signifie
   " Wages, and board, and bed?

* *Twaie coneynge Clerks.*—*Coneynge* is the participle of the
verb to *ken* or *know*. It by no means imports what we now
denominate a *knowing one :* on the contrary, *twaie coneynge
clerks* means *two intelligent and disinterested clergymen.*
† *Seely* is evidently the original of the modern word *silly.*
—A *seely wight*, however, by no means imports what is now
called *a silly fellow*, but means a man of simplicity of character, devoid of all *vanity*, and of any strange ill-conducted
ambition, which, if successful, would immediately be fatal
to the man who indulged it.

D

" And by St. George, that stout horseman,
  " My palfreys *seventeen*,
" For two years, or perchance for three,
  " I had forgotten clean."

" Naie," quoth the Clerk, " both horse and foot
  " To hide was thine intent,
" Ne seely wight be ye, but did
  " With good advisament. *

" Surcharge, surcharge, good Taxing-man,
  " Anon our seals we fix,
" Of sterling pounds, Lord Duke, you pay
  " Three hundred thirty-six."

EPIGRAM

ON THE PARIS LOAN, CALLED

THE LOAN UPON ENGLAND.

THE Paris cits, a patriotic band,
Advance their cash on British freehold land.
But let the speculating rogues beware—
They've bought the *skin*, but who's to kill *the bear?*

* *Good advisament* means—*cool consideration.*

No. IX.

Jan. 8.

ODE TO ANARCHY.

BY A JACOBIN.

(BEING AN IMITATION OF HORACE, ODE 25, BOOK I.)

O Diva, gratum quæ regis Antium!

GODDESS, whose dire terrific power
Spreads, from thy much-loved Gallia's plains,
Where'er her blood-stain'd ensigns lower,
Where'er fell Rapine stalks, or barb'rous Discord reigns!

Thou, who canst lift to fortune's height
The wretch by truth and virtue scorn'd,
And crush, with insolent delight,
All whom true merit raised, or noble birth adorn'd !

Thee, oft the murd'rous band implores,
Swift-darting on its hapless prey:
Thee, wafted from fierce Afric's shores,
The Corsair chief invokes to speed him on his way.

Thee, the wild Indian tribes revere;
Thy charms the roving Arab owns;
Thee, kings, thee, tranquil nations fear,
The bane of social bliss, the foe to peaceful thrones.

For, soon as thy loud trumpet calls
  To deadly rage, to fierce alarms,
  Just order's goodly fabric falls,
Whilst the mad people cries, " to arms! to arms!"

  With thee Proscription, child of strife,
  With death's choice implements, is seen,
  Her murd'rer's gun, assassin's knife,
And, " last not least in love," her darling *Guillotine.*

  Fond hope is thine,—the hope of spoil,
  And faith,—such faith as ruffians keep :
  They prosper thy destructive toil,
That makes the widow mourn, the helpless orphan
    weep.

  Then false and hollow friends retire,
  Nor yield one sigh to soothe despair ;
  Whilst crowds triumphant Vice admire,
Whilst harlots shine in robes that deck'd the great and
    fair.

  Guard our famed chief to Britain's strand !
  Britain, our last, our deadliest foe :
  Oh, guard his brave associate band !
A band to slaughter train'd, and " nursed in scenes
    of woe."

  What shame, alas ! one little Isle
  Should dare its native laws maintain ?

At Gallia's threats serenely smile,
And, scorning her dread power, triumphant rule the
    main.

For this have guiltless victims died
In crowds at thy ensanguined shrine!
For this has recreant Gallia's pride
O'erturn'd religion's fanes, and braved the wrath divine!

What throne, what altar, have we spared
To spread thy power, thy joys impart?
Ah then, our faithful toils reward!
And let each falchion pierce some loyal Briton's heart.

―――――――

*The following Song is recommended to be sung at all convi-
   vial Meetings, convened for the purpose of opposing the
   Assessed Tax Bill. The Correspondent who has transmitted it to us, informs us that he has tried it with great
   success among many of his well disposed neighbours, who
   had been at first led to apprehend that the 120th part of
   their income was too great a sacrifice, for the preservation of the remainder of their property from French Con
   fiscation.*

You have heard of Rewbell,
That demon of hell,
   And of Barras, his brother Director;

Of the canting Lepaux,
And that scoundrel Moreau,
    Who betray'd his old friend and protector.

Would you know how these friends,
For their own private ends,
    Would subvert our religion and throne?—
Do you doubt of their skill
To change laws at their will?—
    You shall hear how they treated their own.

'Twas their pleasure to look,
In a little blue book,
    At the code of their famed legislation,
That with truth they might say,
In the space of one day
    They had broke every law of the nation.

The first law that they see,
Is " *the press shall be free!*"
    The next is " *the trial by jury*:"
Then, " *the people's free choice*;"
Then, " *the members' free voice*"—
    When Rewbell exclaim'd in a fury—

" On a method we'll fall
" For infringing them all—
    " We'll seize on each printer and member :
" No period so fit
" For a desperate hit,
    " As our old bloody month of *September.*

" We'll annul each election
" Which wants our correction,
    " And name our own creatures instead.
" When once we've our will,
" No blood we will spill,
    " (Let Carnot be knock'd on the head).

" To *Rochefort* we'll drive
" Our victims alive,
    " And as soon as on board we have got 'em,
" Since we destine the ship
" For no more than one trip,
    " We can just make a hole in the bottom.

" By this excellent plan,
" On the *true Rights of Man*,
    " When we've founded our *fifth Revolution*,
" Though *England*'s our foe,
" An army shall go
    " To *improve* HER corrupt Constitution.

" We'll address to the nation
" A fine proclamation,
    " With offers of friendship so warm—
" Who can give Buonaparte
" A welcome so hearty
    " As the friends of a THOROUGH REFORM ?''

No. X.

Jan. 15.

For the two following poems we are indebted to unknown Correspondents.

They could not have reached us at a more seasonable period.

The former, we trust, describes the feelings common to every inhabitant of this country. The second, we know too well, is expressive of the sentiments of our enemies.

LINES,

WRITTEN AT THE CLOSE OF THE YEAR 1797.

Loud howls the storm along the neighbouring shore—
BRITAIN indignant hears the frantic roar :
Her generous sons pour forth on every side,
Firm in their country's cause—their country's pride !
See wild invasion threats this envied land :
Swift to defend her, springs each Social Band ;
Her white rocks echoing to their cheerful cry,
" God and our King,"—" England and Victory !"

Yes ! happy BRITAIN, on thy tranquil coast
No trophies mad Philosophy shall boast :

Though thy disloyal sons, a feeble band,
Sound the loud blast of treason through the land:
Scoff at thy dangers with unnatural mirth,
And execrate the soil which gave them birth,
With jaundiced eye thy splendid triumphs view,
And give to FRANCE, the palm to BRITAIN due:
Or,—when loud strains of gratulation ring,
And lowly bending to the ETERNAL KING,
Thy SOVEREIGN bids a nation's praise arise
In grateful incense to the fav'ring skies—
Cast o'er each solemn scene a scornful glance,
And only sigh for ANARCHY and FRANCE.

Yes! unsupported *Treason's* standard falls,
Sedition vainly on her children calls,
While cities, cottages, and camps contend,
Their King, their Laws, their Country to defend.

Raise, BRITAIN, raise thy sea-encircled head,
Round the wide world behold thy glory spread,
Firm as thy guardian oaks thou still shalt stand,
The dread and wonder of each hostile land;
While the dire fiends of discord idly rave,
And, mad with anguish, curse the severing wave.

QUEEN of the OCEAN, lo! she smiles serene,
'Mid the deep horrors of the dreadful scene;
With heartfelt piety to Heav'n she turns—
From Heav'n the flame of British courage burns—

She dreads no power but HIS who rules the ball,
At whose " great bidding" empires, rise and fall ;
In HIM, on peaceful plain, or tented field,
She trusts, secure in HIS protecting shield—
GALLIA, thy threats she scorns—BRITAIN shall never
    yield.

AN ENGLISHWOMAN.

TRANSLATION OF THE NEW SONG

OF THE

"ARMY OF ENGLAND."

WRITTEN BY THE CI-DEVANT BISHOP OF AUTUN.

WITH NOTES BY THE TRANSLATOR.

GOOD Republicans all,
The Directory's call
   Invites you to visit JOHN BULL ;
Oppress'd by the rod
Of a King, and a God,*
   The cup of his misery's full.

* General Danican, in his Memoirs, tells us, that while he was in command, a felon, who had assumed the name of Brutus, Chief of a Revolutionary tribunal at Rennes, said to his colleagues, on Good Friday, " Brothers, we must put to " death this day, at the same hour the Counter-Revolutionist " Christ died, that young devotee who was lately arrested :" and this young lady was guillotined accordingly, and her corpse treated with *every possible species of indecent insult*, to the infinite amusement of a vast multitude of spectators.

Old JOHNNY shall see
What makes a man free ;
 Not parchments, nor statutes on paper ;—
And stripp'd of his riches,
Great charter, and breeches,
 Shall cut a free citizen's caper.

Then away, let us over
To Deal, or to Dover—
 We laugh at his talking so big ;
He's pamper'd with feeding,
And wants a sound bleeding—
 Par Dieu! he shall bleed like a pig !

JOHN, tied to the stake,
A grand baiting will make,
 When worried by mastiffs of France ;
What Republican fun !
To see his blood run,
 As at Lyons, La Vendée, and Nantz.*

* The Reader will find in the works of Peter Porcupine
(a spirited and instructive writer), an ample and satisfactory
commentary on this and the following stanza. The French
themselves inform us, that, by the several modes of destruction here alluded to, upwards of 30,000 persons were but-
chered at Lyons, and this once magnificent city almost levelled
to the ground, by the command of a wretched actor (Collot
d'Herbois), whom they had formerly hissed from the stage.
From the same authorities we learn, that at Nantz 27,000
persons, of both sexes, were murdered ; chiefly by drown-
ing them in plugged-boats. The waters of the Loire became
putrid, and were forbidden to be drank, by the savages who

With grape shot discharges,
And plugs in his barges,
    With *National Razors* good store,
We'll pepper, and shave him,
And in the *Thames* lave him—
    How sweetly he'll bellow and roar!

What the villain likes worse,
We'll vomit his purse,
    And make it the guineas disgorge;
For your Raphaels and Rubens
We would not give two-pence;
    Stick, stick to the PICTURES OF GEORGE.

No Venus of stone,
But of good flesh and bone
    Will do for a true Democrat;
When weary with slaughter,
With JOHN's Wife and Daughter
    We'll join in a little *chit-chat*.

---

conducted the massacre.—That at Paris 150,000, and in La
Vendée 300,000 persons were destroyed.—Upon the whole,
the French themselves acknowledge, that TWO MILLIONS
of human beings (exclusive of the military), have been sacri-
ficed to the principles of EQUALITY and the RIGHTS OF
MAN: 250,000 of these are stated to be WOMEN, and 30,000
CHILDREN. In this last number, however, they do not in-
clude the unborn; nor those who started from the bodies
of their agonizing parents, and were stuck upon the bayonets
of those very men who are now to compose the "ARMY OF
" ENGLAND," amidst the most savage acclamations.

The shop-keeping hoard,
The tenant, and lord,
   And the merchants,* are excellent prey:
At our cannon's first thunder,
Rape, pillage, and *plunder*
   The *Order* shall be *of the day.*

French fortunes and lives,
French daughters and wives,
   Have *five honest men* to defend 'em?
And Barras and Co.
When to England we go,
   Will kindly take JOHN's *in commendam.*

---

* At Lyons, Jabogues, the *second* murderer (the actor being the *first*), in his speech to the Democratic Society, used these words—" Down with the edifices raised for the profit " or the pleasure of the rich; down with them ALL. COM-" MERCE and ARTS are useless to a warlike people, and are " the destruction of that SUBLIME EQUALITY which France " is determined to spread over the globe."

Such are the consequences of RADICAL REFORM!!! Let any merchant, farmer, or landlord: let any husband or father consider this, and then say, " *Shall we or shall we not* " *contribute a moderate sum,* IN PROPORTION TO OUR AN-" NUAL EXPENDITURE, *for the purpose of preserving our-* " *selves from the fate of Lyons, La Vendée, and Nantz.*

                              STYPTIC.

No. XI.

Jan. 22.

We have said in another part of our Paper of this day, " that " though we shall never begin an attack, we shall always " be prompt to repel it."

On this principle, we could not pass over in silence, the Epistle to the Editors of the Anti-Jacobin, which appeared in the Morning Chronicle of Wednesday, and from which we have fortunately been furnished with a Motto for this day's Paper.

We assure the Author of the Epistle, that the Answer which we have here the honour to address to him, contains our genuine and undisguised sentiments upon the merits of the poem.

Our conjectures respecting the authors and abettors of this performance may possibly be as vague and unfounded as theirs are with regard to the Editors of the Anti-Jacobin. We are sorry that we cannot satisfy their curiosity upon this subject—but we have little anxiety for the gratification of our own.

TO THE AUTHOR OF THE
EPISTLE TO THE EDITORS OF THE ANTI-JACOBIN.

Nostrorum sermonum candide judex!

Bard of the borrow'd lyre! to whom belong
The shreds and remnants of each hackney'd song;

* It is hardly to be expected, that the character of the
Epistle should be taken on trust from the Editors of this Volume: it is thought best, therefore, to subjoin the whole
performance as it originally appeared: a mode of hostility
obviously the most fair, and in respect to the combatants in
the cause of Jacobinism, by much the most effectual. They
are always best opposed by the arms which they themselves
furnish. Jacobinism shines by its own light.

To the respectable names which the author of the following Address has thought proper to connect with the " An-
" ti-Jacobin," no apology is made for thus preserving
this otherwise perishable specimen of dullness and defama-
tion. He who has been reviled by the enemies of the " An-
" ti-Jacobin," must feel that principles are attributed to
him, of which he need not be ashamed: and when the abuse
is conveyed in such a strain of feebleness and folly, he must
see that those principles excite animosity only in quarters of
which he need not be afraid.

It is only necessary to add, what is most conscientiously
the truth, that this production, such as it is, is *by far the best*
of all the attacks that the combined wits of the cause have
been able to muster against the " Anti-Jacobin."

EPISTLE
to the
EDITORS OF THE ANTI-JACOBIN.

Hic Niger est; hunc tu, Romane, caveto!

To tell what gen'rals did, or statesmen spoke,
To teach the world by truths, or please by joke:

Whose verse thy friends in vain for wit explore,
And count but *one good line* in eighty-four !

To make mankind grow bold as they peruse,
Judge on existing things, and—weigh the news ;
For this a PAPER first display'd its page,
Commanding tears and smiles through ev'ry age !

   Hail, justly famous ! who in modern days
With nobler flight aspire to higher praise ;
Hail, justly famous ! whose discerning eyes
At once detect MISTAKES, MIS-STATEMENTS, LIES ;
Hail, justly famous ! who, with fancy blest,
Use fiend-like virulence for sportive jest ;
Who only bark to serve your private ends—
Patrons of Prejudice, Corruption's friends !
Who hurl your venom'd darts at well-earn'd fame—
Virtue your hate, and Calumny your aim !

Whoe'er ye are, all hail !—whether the skill
Of youthful C—nn—g guides the ranc'rous quill,
With powers mechanic far above his age
Adapts the paragraph and fills the page,
Measures the column, mends whate'er's amiss,
Rejects THAT letter, and accepts of THIS ;
Or H—mm—d, leaving his official toil,
O'er this great work consume the midnight oil—
Bills, passports, letters, for the Muses quit,
And change dull business for amusing wit :—
His life of labour at one gasp is o'er,
His books forgot—his desk belov'd no more !
Proceed to prop the Ministerial cause ;
See consequential M—rp—th nods applause ;
In ev'ry fair one's ear at balls and plays
The gentle Gr—nv—le L—v—s—n whispers praise :—
Well-judging Patrons, whom such works can please ;
Great works, well worthy Patrons such as these !

Who heard not, raptur'd, the poetic Sage
Who sung of Gallia in a headlong rage,

Whoe'er thou art, all hail ! thy bitter smile
Gilds our dull page, and cheers our humble toil !

And blandly drew with no uncourtly grace
The simple manners of our English race—
Extoll'd great Duncan, and, supremely brave,
Whelm'd Buonaparte's pride beneath the wave ?
I swear by all the youths that M—lm—sb—ry chose,
By Ell—s' sapient prominence of nose,
By M—rp—th's gait important, proud, and big—
By L—s—n G—w'r's crop-imitating wig,
That, could the pow'rs which in those numbers shine,
Could that warm spirit animate my line,
Your glorious deeds which humbly I rehearse—
Your deeds should live immortal as my verse ;
And, while they wonder'd whence I caught my flame,
Your sons should blush to read their father's shame !

    Proceed, great men !—your office is not done ;
Proceed with what you have so well begun :
Load Fox (if you by Pitt would be preferr'd)
With ev'ry guilt that Kenyon ever heard—
Adult'rer, gamester, drunkard, cheat, and knave,
A factious demagogue and pension'd slave !
Loose, loose your cry—with ire satiric flash ;
Let all the Opposition feel your lash,
And prove them to these hot and partial times
A combination of the worst of crimes !

    But softer numbers softer subjects fit :—
In liquid phrases thrill the praise of Pitt ;
Extol in eulogies of candid truth
The Virgin Minister—the Heav'n-born Youth ;
The greatest gift that fate to England gave,
Created to support and born to save ;
Prompt to supply whate'er his country lacks—
Skillful to GAG, and knowing how to TAX !
With him companions meet in order stand—
A firm, compact, and well-appointed band :

E

For *yet*—though firm and fearless in the cause
Of pure religion, liberty, and laws,—
Though truth approved, though fav'ring virtue smiled,
Some doubts remain'd :—we *yet* were *unreviled*.

Thanks to thy zeal ! those doubts at length are o'er!
Thy suffrage crowns our wish !—we ask no more
To stamp with sterling worth each honest line,
Than censure, cloth'd in vapid sense like thine !

But say—in full blown honours dost thou sit
'Midst Brooks's *elders* on the bench of wit,
Where H—re, chief-justice, frames the stern decree, ⎫
While with their learned brother, sages three, ⎬
F—tzp—tr—k, T—wnsh—d, Sh—r—d—n, agree ? ⎭

Or art thou one—THE PARTY's flatter'd fool,
Train'd in Debrett's, or Ridgeway's civic school—

Skill'd to advance or to retreat Dundas,
And bear thick battle on his front of brass ;
Grenville with pond'rous head, which match'd we find
By equal ponderosity behind———

But hold, my Muse ; nor farther these pursue !—
Great Editors, we have digress'd from you ;
From you, to whom our trivial lays belong,
From you, the sole inspirers of our song !
Proceed :—urge on the same vindictive strain,
To gain th' applauses of great M—lm—sb—ry's train ;
With jaundiced eyes the noblest patriot scan ;
Proceed—be more opprobrious if you can ;
Proceed—be more abusive ev'ry hour ;—
To be more stupid is beyond your power.

One, who with rant and nonsense daily wears,
Well-natured R—ch—rds—n! thy patient ears;—
Who sees nor taste nor genius in these times,
Save P—r's *buzz* prose,* and C—rt—ny's kidnapp'd
    rhimes?†

* Buzz Prose.—The learned reader will perceive that
this is an elegant *metonymy*, by which the quality belonging
to the outside of the head is transferred to the inside. *Buzz*
is an epithet usually applied to a large wig. It is here used
for swelling, burly, bombastic writing.

There is a picture of Hogarth's (the Election Ball, we believe), in which among a number of hats thrown together in
one corner of the room, there is not one, of which you cannot
to a certainty point out the owner among the figures dancing,
or otherwise distributed through the picture.

We remember to have seen an experiment of this kind
tried at one of the Universities with the *wig* and *writings*
here alluded to. A page taken from the most happy and
elaborate part of the writings, was laid upon a table in a bar-
ber's shop, round which a number of wigs of different de-
scriptions and dimensions were suspended, and among them
that of the Author of the writings. It was required of a young
student, after reading a few sentences in the page, to point
out among the wigs, that which must of necessity belong to
the head in which such sentences had been engendered. The
experiment succeeded to a miracle.—The learned reader
will now see all the beauty and propriety of the *metonymy*.

† Kidnapp'd Rhimes.—Kidnapp'd, implies something
more than *stolen*. It is, according to an expression of Mr.
Sheridan's (in the *Critic*) using *other people's* "*thoughts as gip-
"sies do stolen children—disfiguring them, to make them pass for
"their own.*"

This is a serious charge against an Author, and ought to
be well supported. To the proof then!

In an Ode of the late Lord Nugent's, are the following
spirited lines:

Or is it he,—the youth, whose daring soul
With *half a mission* sought the Frozen Pole ;—
And then, returning from the unfinish'd work,
Wrote *half a letter*,—to demolish Burke ?
Studied Burke's manner,—aped his forms of speech ;—
Though when he strives his metaphors to reach,

    " Though Cato liv'd—though Tully spoke —
    " Though Brutus dealt the godlike stroke,
      " Yet perish'd fated Rome !''

The Author above mentioned, saw these lines, and liked them—as well he might : and as he had a mind to write about Rome himself, he did not scruple to enlist them into his service ; but he thought it right to make a small alteration in their appearance, which he managed thus—Speaking of Rome, he says it is the place

    " *Where* Cato liv'd ''—

A sober truth : which gets rid at once of all the poetry and spirit of the original, and reduces the sentiment from an example of manners, virtue, patriotism, from the *vitæ exemplar dedit* of Lord Nugent, to a mere question of inhabitancy. *Ubi habitavit Cato* —where he was an inhabitant-house-holder, paying scot and lot, and had a house on the right-hand side of the way, as you go down *Esquiline* Hill, just opposite to the poulterer's—But to proceed—

    " *Where* Cato liv'd ; *where* Tully spoke,
    " *Where* Brutus dealt the godlike stroke —
  ——— " *By which his glory rose ! ! !*''

The last line is *not* borrowed.
We question whether the History of modern Literature can produce an instance of a theft so shameless, and turned to so little advantage.

One luckless slip his meaning overstrains,
And loads the blunderbuss with B—df—d's brains.*

---

* *And loads the blunderbuss with B—df—d's brains*—This
line is wholly unintelligible without a note. And we are
afraid the note will be wholly incredible, unless the reader
can fortunately procure the book to which it refers.

In the " Part of a Letter," which was published by Mr.
Robt. Ad—r, in answer to Mr. Burke's " Letter to the D.
of B." nothing is so remarkable as the studious imitation of
Mr. Burke's *style*.

His vehemence, and his passion, and his irony, his wild
imagery, his far-sought illustrations, his rolling and length-
ened periods, and the short quick pointed sentences in which
he often condenses as much wisdom and wit as others would
expand through pages, or through volumes—all these are
carefully kept in view by his opponent, though not always
very artificially copied or applied.

But imitators are liable to be led strangely astray : and
never was there an instance of a more complete mistake of
a plain meaning, than that which this line is intended to illustrate—a mistake no less than of a *coffin* for a *corpse*. This
is hard to believe, or to comprehend—but you shall hear.

Mr. Burke, in one of his publications, had talked of the
French " *unplumbing* the dead in order to destroy the living,"—by which he intended, without doubt, not meta-
phorically, but literally, *stripping the dead of their leaden coffins, and then making them (not the* DEAD, *but the* COFFINS)
into bullets."—A circumstance perfectly notorious at the time
the book was written.

But this does not satisfy our Author. He determines to
retort Mr. Burke's own words upon him ; and unfortunately
" reaching at a metaphor," where Mr. Burke only intended
a fact, he falls into the little mistake above mentioned, and
by a stroke of his pen, transmutes the illustrious Head of the
house of Russell into a metal, to which it is not for us to
say how near, or how remote his affinity may possibly have
been—He writes thus—" *If Mr. Burke had been content with
' unplumbing' a dead Russell, and hewing* HIM (observe—not

Whoe'er thou art—ne'er may thy patriot fire,
Unfed by praise or patronage, expire!
Forbid it, Taste!—with compensation large
Patrician hands thy labours shall o'ercharge! *
B—df—rd and Wh—tbr—d shall vast sums advance,
The *Land and Malt* of Jacobin Finance!

Whoe'er thou art!—before thy feet we lay,
With lowly suit, our *Number of to-day!*
Spurn not our offering with averted eyes!
Let thy pure breath revive the extinguish'd *Lies!*
Mistakes, Mis-statements, now so oft o'erthrown,
Rebuild, and prop with nonsense of thy own!
Pervert our meaning, and misquote our text—
And *furnish us a motto for the next!*

the coffin, but HIM—the old dead Russell himself) *into grape
and canister, to sweep down the whole generation of his descen-
dants,*" &c. &c. &c.
     The thing is scarcely credible: but it is so! We write
with the book open before us.
     * Qu.—Surcharge?

ODE TO LORD M—RA.

I.

IF on your head * some vengeance fell,
M—ra for every tale you tell
  The listening Lords to cozen ;
If but one whisker lost its hue,
Chang'd (like Moll Coggin's tail) to blue,
  I'd hear them by the dozen.

II.

But still, howe'er you draw your bow,†
Your charms improve, your triumphs grow,
  New grace adorns your figure ;
More stiff your boots, more black your stock,
Your hat assumes a prouder cock,
  Like Pistol's (if 'twere bigger.)

HORACE.   ODE VIII.   BOOK II.

IN BARINEN.

  * *Ulla si juris tibi pejerati*
    Pœna, Barine, nocuisset unquam;
    Dente si nigro fieres, vel uno
                    Turpior ungui,

  Crederem. † *Sed tu simul obligásti*
  Perfidum votis caput, enitescis
  Pulchrior multo, juvenumque prodis
                    Publica cura.

III.

Tell then your stories, strange and new,
Your Father's fame* shall vouch them true ;
 So shall the *Dublin Papers* :
Swear by the stars † that saw the sight,
That infant thousands die each night,
 While troops *blow out their tapers*.

IV.

Sh—br—h ‡ shall cheer you with a smile,
M—cph—rs—n § simpering all the while,
 With B—st—rd § and with Bruin : §
And fierce N—ch—ll,‖ who wields at will
Th' emphatic stick, or powerful quill,
 To prove his country's ruin.

V.

Each day new followers ¶ crowd your board,
And lean expectants hail my Lord

  * Expedit *matris cineres* opertos
  Fallere, et toto † *taciturna noctis*
  Signa cum cœlo, gelidâque Divos
       Morte carentes.

  Ridet hoc, inquam, ‡ Venus ipsa, rident
  Simplices § Nymphæ; ferus et ‖ Cupido,
  Semper ardentes acuens sagittas
       Cote cruentâ.

  Adde quod pubes tibi crescit omnis
  ¶ *Servitus crescit nova ;*————

With adoration fervent :
Old Th—rl—w,* though he swore by G—
No more to own a master's nod,
  Is still your humble servant.

VI.

Old P—lt—n—y † too your influence feels,
And asks from you th' Exchequer seals,
  To tax and save the nation :
T—ke trembles,** lest your potent charms
Should lure C—s F—x ‡ from *his* fond arms,
  To your Administration.

---

* ——————————— *nec priores*
Impiæ tectum dominæ relinquunt
            Sæpe minati.

Te suis matres metuunt juvencis
Te † *senes parci, miseræque* ‡ *nuper*
Virgines nuptæ, tua ne retardet
            Aura Maritos.

** The trepidation of Mr. T—ke, though natural, was not
necessary ; as it appeared from the ever-memorable " Letter
" to Mr. MacMahon," (which was published about this time
in the *Morning Chronicle*, and threw the whole town into pa-
roxysms of laughter) that in the Administration which his
Lordship was so gravely employed in forming, Mr. Fox was
to have no place !

No. XII.

Jan. 29.

The following Ode was dropped into the letter-box in our
Publisher's window.   From its title—" A BIT OF AN
" ODE TO MR. FOX"—we were led to imagine there
was some mistake in the business, and that it was meant
to have been conveyed to Mr. Wright's neighbour, Mr.
Debrett, whom we recollected to have been the Publisher
of the " Half of a Letter" to the same Gentleman, which
occasioned so much noise (of horse-laughing) in the world.
Our politics certainly do not entitle us to the honourable
distinction of being made the channel for communicating
such a production to the public.   But, for our parts, as we
are " not at war with Genius," on whatever side we find
it, we are happy to give this Poem the earliest place in our
Paper ;   and shall be equally ready to pay the same atten-
tion to any future favours of the same kind, and from the
same quarter.

The Poem is a free translation, or rather, perhaps, imita-
tion, of the 20th Ode of the 2d Book of Horace.   We have
taken the liberty to subjoin the passages of which the pa-
rallel is the most striking.

A BIT OF AN ODE TO MR. FOX.

I.

On * grey goose quills sublime I'll soar,
To metaphors unreach'd before,
    That scare the vulgar reader :
With style well form'd from Burke's best books—
From rules of grammar (e'en Horne Tooke's)
    A bold and free Seceder.

II.

I † whom, dear Fox, you condescend
To call your Honourable Friend,
    Shall live for everlasting :
That ‡ Stygian gallery I'll quit,
Where Printers crowd me as I sit
    Half-dead with rage and fasting.

III.

I § feel ! the growing down descends,
Like goose-skin, to my fingers' ends—

---

* Non usitatâ nec tenui ferar
    Pennâ, biformis per liquidum æthera
    Vates.
† ———— Non ego, quam vocas
    Dilecte, Mæcenas, obibo,
‡ Nec Stygiâ cohibebor undâ.
§ Jamjam residunt cruribus asperæ
    Pelles : et album mutor in alitem

Each nail becomes a feather:
My * cropp'd head waves with sudden plumes,
Which erst (like B—df—rd's, or his groom's)
    Unpowder'd, brav'd the weather.

IV.

I mount, I mount into the sky,
" Sweet † bird," to ‡ Petersburg I'll fly:
    Or, if you bid, to Paris ;
Fresh missions of the *Fox* and *goose*
Successful treaties may produce ;
    Though Pitt in all miscarries.

V.

Scotch, § English, Irish *Whigs* shall read
The pamphlets, letters, odes I breed,
    Charm'd with each bright endeavour :
Alarmists ‖ tremble at my strain,
E'en ¶ Pitt, made candid by champaign,
    Shall hail Ad—r " *the clever.*"

---

    * Supernè ; nascunturque læves
      Per digitos humerosque plumæ.
    . . . .
    Visam gementis littora Bosphori,
    Syrtesque Gætulas, † canorus
      Ales, ‡ Hyperboreosque campos.
    § Me Colchus, et qui ‖ dissimulat metum.
    . . . .
    . . . . me peritus
    Discet Iber, Rhodanique ¶ potor.

VI.

Though criticism assail my name,
And luckless blunders blot my * fame,
   O ! † make no needless bustle ;
As vain and idle it would be
To waste one pitying thought on me,
   As to ‡ " unplumb a R—ss—ll."

    Absint * inani funere nænia.
  † Luctusque turpes, et querimoniæ.
  ‡ ————— ————— sepulchri
    Mitte supervacuos honores.

No. XIII.

Feb. 5.

ACME AND SEPTIMIUS;

OR,

THE HAPPY UNION.

CELEBRATED AT THE CROWN AND ANCHOR TAVERN.

Fox,* with Tooke to grace his side,
Thus address'd his blooming bride—
" Sweet! should I e'er, in power or place,
" Another Citizen embrace ;
" Should e'er my eyes delight to look
" On aught alive, save John Horne Tooke,
" Doom me to ridicule and ruin,
" In the coarse hug † of *Indian* Bruin ! "

    He spoke;‡ and to the left and right,
N—rf—lk hiccupp'd with delight.

       * Acmen Septimius suos amores
         Tenens in gremio, mea, inquit, Acme,
         Ni te perdite amo, &c.
       † Cæsio veniam obvius Leoni.
       ‡ Hoc ut dixit, Amor sinistram, ut
         Dextram, sternuit approbationem.

Tooke,* his bald head gently moving,
   On the sweet Patriot's drunken eyes,
   His wine-empurpled lips applies,
And thus returns in accents loving :

" So, my dear † Charley, may success
" At length my ardent wishes bless,
" And lead, through Discord's low'ring storm,
" To one grand RADICAL REFORM !
" As, from this hour I love thee more
" Than e'er I hated thee before !"

   He spoke,‡ and to the left and right,
   N—rf—lk hiccupp'd with delight.

With this good omen they proceed; §
Fond toasts their mutual passion feed ;
In Fox's breast Horne Tooke prevails
Before ‖ rich *Ireland* ** and *South Wales;* **

---

  * At Acme leviter caput reflectens,
    Et dulcis pueri ebrios ocellos
    Illo purpureo ore suaviata.
    Sic, inquit, mea vita, † Septimille, &c.
  ‡ Hoc ut dixit, Amor sinistram, &c.
  § Nunc ab auspicio bono profecti
    Mutuis animis amant, amantur.
    Unam Septimius misellus Acmen
    Mavult quam ‖ Syrias Britanniasque.

  ** *i. e.* The Clerkship of the Pells in Ireland, and Audi-
torship of South Wales.

And Fox (un-read each other book),
Is Law and Gospel to Horne Tooke.

When were such kindred souls * united !
Or wedded pair so much delighted ?

    * Quis ullos homines beatiores
      Vidit, quis venerem auspicatiorem ?

No. XIV.

Feb. 12.

It has been our invariable custom to suppress such of our Correspondents' favours as conveyed any Compliments to ourselves; and we have deviated from it in the present instance, not so much out of respect to the uncommon excellence of the Poem before us, as because it agrees so intimately with the general design of our Paper, to expose the deformity of the French Revolution, to counteract the detestable arts of those who are seeking to introduce it here, and above all, to invigorate the exertions of our Countrymen against every Foe, foreign and domestic, by shewing them the immense and inexhaustible resources they yet possess in British Courage and British Virtue!

TO THE AUTHOR
OF THE ANTI-JACOBIN.

Foe to thy country's foes! 'tis THINE to claim
From Britain's genuine sons a British fame—
Too long French manners our fair isle disgraced;
Too long French fashions shamed our native taste.
Still prone to change, we half-resolved to try
The proffer'd charms of FRENCH FRATERNITY.

F

Fair was her form, and FREEDOM's honour'd name
Conceal'd the horrors of her secret shame :
She claim'd some kindred with that guardian pow'r,
Long worshipp'd here in Britain's happier hour :
Virtue and peace, she said, were in her train,
The long-lost blessings of Astræa's reign—
But soon the vizor dropp'd—her haggard face
Betray'd the Fury lurking in the Grace—
The false attendants that behind her press'd,
In vain disguised, the latent guilt confess'd :
PEACE dropt her snow-white robe, and shudd'ring
        shew'd
AMBITION's mantle reeking fresh with blood ;
Presumptuous FOLLY stood in REASON's form,
Pleas'd with the power to ruin,—not reform ;
PHILOSOPHY, proud phantom, undismay'd,
With cold regard the ghastly train survey'd ;
Saw PERSECUTION gnash her iron teeth,
While Atheists preach'd the *eternal sleep of death* ;
Saw ANARCHY the social chain unbind,
And DISCORD sour the blood of humankind ;
Then talk'd of Nature's Rights, and Equal Sway ;
And saw her system safe—and stalk'd away !

Foil'd by our ARMS, where'er in arms we met,
With ARTS LIKE THESE, the foe assails us yet.
Hopeless the fort to storm, or to surprise,
More secret wiles his envious malice tries ;
Diseas'd himself, spreads wide his own despair,
Pollutes the fount, and taints the wholesome air.

While many a chief, to glory not unknown,
Alarms each hostile shore, and guards our own,
'Tis THINE, the latent treachery to proclaim;
An humbler warfare, but the cause the same.
In vain had Pompey crush'd the Pontic host,
And chas'd the pirate swarm from every coast;
Had not the Civic Consul's watchful eye
Track'd through the windings of conspiracy,
The crew that leagued their country to o'erthrow;
The base confederates of a Gallic * foe;
Expos'd, confounded, sham'd, and forc'd away,
The "JACOBIN REFORMER † of his day."

'Tis THINE a subtler mischief to pursue,
And drag a deeper, darker, plot to view;
Whate'er its form, still ready to engage,
Detect its malice, or resist its rage;
Whether it whispers low, or raves aloud,
In sneers profane, or blasphemies avow'd;
Insults its King, reviles its Country's cause,
And, 'scaped from justice, braves the lenient laws:—
Whate'er the hand in desperate faction bold,
By native hate inspir'd, or foreign gold;

* Conjuravere Cives noblissimi Patriam incendere—*Gallorum* gentem infestissimam nomini Romano in bellum arcessunt—Dux Hostium cum exercitu supra caput est.—ORAT. CATON. ap. SALLUST.
† Tum Catalina polliceri tabulas novas, proscriptionem locupletium, Magistratus, Sacerdotia, rapinas, alia omnia quæ bellum atque lubido Victorum fert.—SALLUST.

Traitors absolv'd, and libellers releas'd,
The recreant peer, or renegado priest;
The *Sovereign-people*'s cringing, crafty slave,
The dashing fool, and instigating knave,
Each claims thy care; nor think the labour vain;
Vermin have sunk the Ship that ruled the Main.

'Tis THINE, with truth's fair shield to ward the blow,
And turn the weapon back upon the foe:
To trace the skulking fraud, the candid cheat,
That can retract the falsehood, yet repeat:
To wake the listless, slumb'ring as they lie,
Lapt in the embrace of soft security;
To rouse the cold, re-animate the brave,
And shew the cautious ALL THEY HAVE TO SAVE.

Erect that standard ALFRED first unfurl'd,
Britain's just pride, the wonder of the world;
Whose staff is Freedom's spear, whose blazon'd field
Beams with the CHRISTIAN CROSS, the REGAL
    SHIELD;
That standard, which the Patriot Barons bore,
Restor'd, from Runimede's resounding shore;
Which since consign'd to William's guardian hand,
Wav'd in new splendour o'er a grateful land;
Which oft in vain by force or fraud assail'd,
Has stood the shock of ages—and prevail'd.

Yes!—the BRIGHT SUN OF BRITAIN yet shall shine,
The clouds are earthborn, but his fire divine;

That temperate splendour, and that genial heat,
Shall still illume, and cherish empire's seat;
While the red meteor, whose portentous glare
Shot plagues infectious through the troubled air;
Admir'd, or fear'd no more, shall melt away,
Lost in the radiance of HIS BRIGHTER DAY!

———

LINES

WRITTEN UNDER THE BUST OF CHARLES FOX,

AT THE CROWN AND ANCHOR.

I'll not sell Uncle Noll, Charles Surface cries;—
I'll not sell Charley Fox, John Bull replies:
Sell him, indeed! who'll find me such another?—
Fox is above all price; so hold your bother.

Morning Post, Feb. 6.

———

To make our Readers some amends for this miser-
able doggrel, we will present them, in our turn, with
some lines written *under a bust*, NOT *at the Crown and
Anchor*, by an English traveller. We believe they are
more just; we are certain they are more poetical.

LINES

*Written by a Traveller at Czarco-zelo under the Bust of a
certain Orator, once placed between those of Demosthenes
and Cicero.*

I.

The Grecian Orator of old,
With scorn rejected Philip's laws,
   Indignant spurn'd at foreign gold,
And triumph'd in his country's cause.

II.

   A foe to every wild extreme,
'Mid civil storms, the Roman Sage
   Repress'd Ambition's frantic scheme,
And check'd the madding people's rage.

III.

   Their country's peace, and wealth, and fame,
With patriot zeal their labours sought,
   And Rome's or Athens' honour'd name
Inspired and govern'd every thought.

IV.

   Who now, in this presumptuous hour,
Aspires to share the Athenian's praise?
   —The advocate of foreign power,
The Æschines of later days.

V.

What chosen name to Tully's join'd,
Is thus announced to distant climes?
  —Behold, to lasting shame consign'd,
The Catiline of modern times!

No. XV.

Feb. 19.

THE PROGRESS OF MAN.

A DIDACTIC POEM.

IN FORTY CANTOS, WITH NOTES CRITICAL AND
EXPLANATORY: CHIEFLY OF A PHILOSO-
PHICAL TENDENCY.

DEDICATED TO R. P. KNIGHT, ESQ.

CANTO FIRST.

CONTENTS.

*The Subject proposed.—Doubts and Waverings.— Queries
not to be answered.— Formation of the stupendous Whole.
—Cosmogony; or the Creation of the World:—the Devil—
Man—Various Classes of Being:—*ANIMATED BEINGS
*—Birds—Fish—Beasts—the Influence of the Sexual Ap-
petite—on Tigers—on Whales—on Crimpt Cod—on Perch
—on Shrimps— on Oysters.—Various Stations assigned to
different Animals :—Birds—Bears—Mackarel.—Bears
remarkable for their fur—Mackarel cried on a Sunday—
Birds do not graze—nor Fishes fly—nor Beasts live in the
Water.—Plants equally contented with their lot :—Potatoes — Cabbage—Lettuce—Leeks—Cucumbers.—*MAN

only discontented—born a Savage; not choosing to con-
tinue so, becomes polished—resigns his Liberty—Priest-
craft—King-craft—Tyranny of Laws and Institutions.
—Savage Life—description thereof:—The Savage free
—roaming Woods—feeds on Hips and Haws—Animal
Food—first notion of it from seeing a Tiger tearing his
prey—wonders if it is good—resolves to try—makes a Bow
and Arrow—kills a Pig—resolves to roast a part of it—
*lights a fire—*APOSTROPHE *to Fires—Spits and Jacks*
*not yet invented. — Digression.—*CORINTH — SHEF-
FIELD. — *Love the most natural desire after Food.—*
Savage Courtship.—Concubinage recommended.—Satirical
Reflections on Parents and Children—Husbands and Wives
*—against collateral Consanguinity.—*FREEDOM *the only*
Morality, &c. &c. &c.

WHETHER some great, supreme o'er-ruling Power
Stretch'd forth its arm at nature's natal hour,
Composed this mighty whole with plastic skill,
Wielding the jarring elements at will?
Or whether sprung from Chaos' mingling storm,   5
The mass of matter started into form?

Ver. 3. A modern Author of great penetration and judgment, observes very shrewdly, that " the Cosmogony of the
" world, has puzzled the philosophers of all ages.   What a
" medley of opinions have they not broached upon the crea-
" tion of the world? Sanconiathon, Manetho, Berosus, and
" Ocellus Lucanus, have all attempted it in vain.   The lat-
" ter has these words—*Anarchon ara kai ateleutaion to pan*—
" which imply, that, all things have neither beginning nor
" end." See Goldsmith's Vicar of Wakefield; see also Mr.
Knight's Poem on the Progress of Civil Society.

Or Chance o'er earth's green lap spontaneous fling
The fruits of autumn and the flowers of spring?
Whether material substance unrefined,
Owns the strong impulse of instinctive mind,   10
Which to one centre points diverging lines,
Confounds, refracts, invig'rates, and combines?
Whether the joys of earth, the hopes of heaven,
By Man to God, or God to Man, were given?
If virtue leads to bliss, or vice to woe?   15
Who rules above? or who reside below?
Vain questions all—shall Man presume to know?
On all these points, and points obscure as these,
Think they who will,—and think whate'er they please!

    Let us a plainer, steadier theme pursue—   20
Mark the grim savage scoop his light canoe;
Mark the dark rook, on pendant branches hung,
With anxious fondness feed her cawing young.—
Mark the fell leopard through the desert prowl,
Fish prey on fish, and fowl regale on fowl;—   25

Ver. 12. The influence of Mind upon Matter, comprehending the whole question of the Existence of Mind as in-
dependent of Matter, or as co-existent with it, and of Matter considered as an intelligent and self-dependent Essence,
will make the subject of a larger Poem in 127 Books, now
preparing under the *same* auspices.
  Ver. 14. See Godwin's Enquirer; Darwin's Zoonomia;
Paine; Priestley, &c. &c. &c.; also all the French Encyclopedists.
  Ver. 16. *Quæstio spinosa et contortula.*

How Lybian tigers' chawdrons love assails,
And warms, midst seas of ice, the melting whales;—
Cools the crimpt cod, fierce pangs to perch imparts,
Shrinks shrivell'd shrimps, but opens oysters' hearts;—
Then say, how all these things together tend   30
To one great truth, prime object, and good end?

    First—to each living thing, whate'er its kind,
Some lot, some part, some station is assign'd.
The feather'd race with pinions skim the *air*—
Not so the mackarel, and still less the bear: 35
This roams the *wood*, carniv'rous, for his prey;
That with soft roe, pursues his *watery* way:—
This slain by hunters, yields his shaggy hide;
That, caught by fishers, is on *Sundays* cried.—

    But each contented with his humble sphere,   40
Moves unambitious through the circling year;

Ver. 26. "Add thereto a tiger's chawdron."—Macbeth.
Ver. 26, 27. "In softer notes bids Lybian lions roar,
  "And warms the whale on Zembla's frozen shore."
               Progress of Civil Society, Book 1. ver. 98.
Ver. 29. "An oyster may be cross'd in love."—Mr. She-
ridan's Critic.
Ver. 34. Birds fly.
Ver. 35. But neither fish, nor beasts—particularly as here
exemplified.
Ver. 36. The bear.
Ver. 37. The mackarel—There are also *hard-roed* macka-
rel. *Sed de his alio loco.*
Ver. 38. Bear's *grease*, or *fat*, is also in great request; being
supposed to have a *crinipdrous*, or hair-producing quality.
Ver. 39. There is a special Act of Parliament which per-
mits mackarel to be cried on Sundays.

Nor e'er forgets the fortune of his race,
Nor pines to quit, or strives to change, his place.
Ah! who has seen the mailed lobster rise,
Clap her broad wings, and soaring claim the skies ? 45
When did the owl, descending from her bow'r
Crop, 'midst the fleecy flocks, the tender flow'r ;
Or the young heifer plunge, with pliant limb,
In the salt wave, and fish-like strive to swim ?

The same with plants—potatoes 'tatoes breed — 50 ⎫
Uncostly cabbage springs from cabbage seed ;   ⎬
Lettuce to lettuce, leeks to leeks succeed ;   ⎭
Nor e'er did cooling cucumbers presume
To flow'r like myrtle, or like violets bloom.
—Man, only,—rash, refined, presumptuous Man, 55
Starts from his rank, and mars creation's plan.

Ver. 45 to 49. Every animal contented with the lot which
it has drawn in life. A fine contrast to man, who is always
discontented.
Ver. 49. *Salt wave*—wave of the sea—" *briny wave.*"—
Poetæ passim.
Ver. 50. A still stronger contrast, and a greater shame to
man, is found in plants ;—they are contented—he restless
and changing. *Mens agitat mihi, nec placidâ contenta quiete est.*
Ver. 50. *Potatoes 'tatoes breed.* Elision for the sake of verse,
not meant to imply that the root degenerates.—Not so with
Man—

Mox daturus
Progeniem vitiosiorem.

Born the free heir of nature's wide domain,
To art's strict limits bounds his narrow'd reign;
Resigns his native rights for meaner things,   59
For Faith and Fetters—Laws, and Priests, and Kings.
(To be continued.)

We are sorry to be obliged to break off here.—The
remainder of this admirable and instructive Poem is in
the press, and will be continued the first opportunity.

THE EDITOR.

No. XVI.

Feb. 26.

THE Specimen of the poem on the " Progress of
Man," with which we favoured our Readers in our
last Number, has occasioned a variety of letters, which
we confess have not a little surprised us, from the
unfounded, and even contradictory charges they contain. In one, we are accused of malevolence, in bringing back to notice a work that had been quietly con-
signed to oblivion;—in another, of plagiarism, in
copying its most beautiful passages;—in a third, of
vanity, in striving to imitate what was in itself ini-
mitable, &c. &c. But why this alarm? has the author
of the *Progress of Civil Society* an exclusive patent for
fabricating *Didactic* poems? or can we not write against
order and government, without incurring the guilt of
imitation? We trust we were not so ignorant of the
nature of a didactic poem (so called from *didaskein*, to
teach, and *poema*, a poem; because it teaches nothing,
and is not poetical) even before the *Progress of Civil
Society* appeared, but that we were capable of such an
undertaking.

We shall only say farther, that we do not intend to
proceed regularly with our poem; but having the re-
maining thirty-nine Cantos by us, shall content our-

selves with giving, from time to time, such extracts as
may happen to suit our purpose.

The following passage, which, as the Reader will see
by turning to the Contents prefixed to the head of the
Poem, is part of the First Canto, contains so happy a
deduction of Man's present state of depravity, from
the first slips and failings of his original state, and in-
culcates so forcibly the mischievous consequences of
social or *civilized,* as opposed to *natural* society, that no
dread of imputed imitation can prevent us from giving
it to our Readers.

PROGRESS OF MAN.

Lo! the rude savage, free from civil strife,
Keeps the smooth tenour of his guiltless life ;
Restrain'd by none, save Nature's lenient laws,
Quaffs the clear stream, and feeds on hips and haws.
Light to his daily sports behold him rise !   65
The bloodless banquet health and strength supplies.
Bloodless not long—one morn he haps to stray
Through the lone wood—and close beside the way
Sees the gaunt tiger tear his trembling prey ;

Ver. 61—66. Simple state of savage life—previous to the
pastoral, or even the hunter state.
Ver. 66. First savages disciples of Pythagoras.
Ver. 67, *&c.* Desire of animal food natural only to beasts,

Beneath whose gory fangs a leveret bleeds,   70
Or pig—such pig as fertile China breeds.

    Struck with the sight, the wondering Savage stands,
Rolls his broad eyes, and clasps his lifted hands;
Then restless roams—and loaths his wonted food;
Shuns the salubrious stream, and thirsts for blood. 75

    By thought matur'd, and quicken'd by desire,
New arts, new arms, his wayward wants require.
From the tough yew a slender branch he tears,
With self-taught skill the twisted grass prepares;
The' unfashion'd bow with labouring efforts bends 80
In circling form, and joins the' unwilling ends.
Next some tall reed he seeks—with sharp-edg'd stone
Shapes the fell dart, and points with whiten'd bone.

    Then forth he fares.   Around in careless play,
Kids, pigs, and lambkins unsuspecting stray.   85
With grim delight he views the sportive band,
Intent on blood, and lifts his murderous hand.

or to man in a state of civilized society. First suggested by
the circumstance here related.
    Ver. 71. Pigs of the *Chinese* breed most in request.
    Ver. 76. First formation of a bow.   Introduction to the
science of archery.
    Ver. 79. Grass twisted, used for a string, owing to the want
of other materials not yet invented.
    Ver. 83. Bone—fish's bone found on the sea-shore, shark's
teeth, &c. &c.

Twangs the bent bow—resounds the fateful dart,
Swift-wing'd, and trembles in a porker's heart.

Ah! hapless porker! what can now avail   90
Thy back's stiff bristles, or thy curly tail?
Ah! what avail those eyes so small and round,
Long pendent ears, and snout that loves the ground?

Not unreveng'd thou diest!—In after times   94
From thy spilt blood shall spring unnumber'd crimes.
Soon shall the slaught'rous arms that wrought thy woe,
Improv'd by malice, deal a deadlier blow;
When *social* Man shall pant for nobler game,
And 'gainst his fellow man the vengeful weapon aim.

As love, as gold, as jealousy inspires,   100
As wrathful hate, or wild ambition fires,
Urged by the stateman's craft, the tyrant's rage,
Embattled nations endless wars shall wage,
Vast seas of blood the ravaged field shall stain,
And millions perish—that a *King* may reign!   105

Ver. 90. Ah! what avails, &c.—See Pope's Description
of the Death of a Pheasant.
Ver. 93. " With leaden eye that loves the ground."
Ver. 94. The first effusion of blood attended with the most
dreadful consequences to mankind.
Ver. 97. *Social* Man's wickedness opposed to the simpli-
city of savage life.
Ver. 100 and 101. Different causes of war among men.

G

For blood once shed, new wants and wishes rise ;
Each rising want invention quick supplies.
To roast his victuals is Man's next desire,
So two dry sticks he rubs, and lights a fire ;
Hail fire ! &c. &c.

Ver. 106. Invention of fire—first employed in cookery,
and produced by rubbing dry sticks together.

No. XVII.

March 5.

We are obliged to a learned Correspondent for the following ingenious imitation of Bion.—We will not
shock the eyes of our Fair Readers with the original
Greek, but the following *Argument* will give them
some idea of the nature of the Poem here imitated.

ARGUMENT.

*Venus is represented as bringing to the Poet, while sleeping,
her son Cupid, with a request that he would teach him
Pastoral Poetry—Bion complies, and endeavours to teach
him the rise and progress of that art :—Cupid laughs at
his instructions, and in his turn teaches his master the
Loves of Men and Gods, the Wiles of his Mother, &c.—
Pleased with his lessons, says Bion, I forgot what I lately
taught Cupid, and recollect in its stead, only what Cupid
taught me.*

IMITATION, &c.

Written at St. Ann's Hill.

Scarce had sleep my eyes o'erspread,
Ere Alecto sought my bed ;
In her left hand a torch she shook,
And in her right led J—n H—ne T—ke.

O thou! who well deserv'st the bays,
Teach him, she cried, Sedition's lays—
She said, and left us; I, poor fool,
Began the wily priest to school;
Taught him how M—ra sung of lights
Blown out by troops o' stormy nights;
How E—sk—e, borne on rapture's wings,
At clubs and taverns sweetly sings
Of *self*—while yawning Whigs attend—
Self first, last, midst, and without end;
How B—df—d piped, ill-fated Bard!
Half-drown'd, in empty Palace-yard;
How L—sd—ne, nature's simple child,
At *B—w—d* trills his wood-notes wild—
How these and more (a phrenzied choir)
Sweep with bold hand Confusion's lyre,
Till madding crowds around them storm
" FOR ONE GRAND RADICAL REFORM!"

T—ke stood silent for a while,
Listening with sarcastic smile;
Then in verse of calmest flow,
Sung of treasons, deep and low,
Of rapine, prisons, scaffolds, blood,
Of war against the great and good;
Of Venice, and of Genoa's doom,
And fall of unoffending Rome;
Of monarchs from their station hurl'd,
And one waste desolated world.

Charm'd by the magic of his tongue,
I lost the strains I lately sung,
While those he taught, remain impress'd
For ever on my faithful breast.

                              DORUS.

───────────

Something like the same idea seems to have dictated the fol-
lowing Stanzas, which appear to be a loose Imitation of
the beautiful Dialogue of Horace and Lydia, and for
which, though confessedly in a lower style of poetry, and
conceived rather in the slang, *or Brentford* dialect, *than*
in the classical Doric of the foregoing Poem, we have
many thanks to return to an ingenious academical Corres-
pondent.

THE NEW COALITION.

I.

F. WHEN erst I coalesced with North,
And brought my *Indian bantling* forth,
In place—I smil'd at faction's storm,
Nor dreamt of *radical Reform.*

II.

T. While yet no patriot project pushing,
Content I thump'd Old Brentford's cushion,
I pass'd my life so free and gaily;
Not dreaming of that d——d *Old Bailey.*

III.

F. Well! now my favourite preacher's *Nickle,*
He keeps for Pitt a rod in pickle;
His gestures fright the' astonish'd gazers,
His sarcasms cut like Packwood's razors.

IV.

T. *Thelwall*'s my man for state alarm;
I love the rebels of *Chalk Farm;*
Rogues that no statutes can subdue,
Who'd bring the French, and head them too.

V.

F. A whisper in your ear, J——n H——ne,
For *one great end* we both were born,
Alike we roar, and rant, and bellow—
Give us your hand, my honest fellow.

VI.

T. Charles, for a shuffler long I've known thee:
But come—for once, I'll not disown thee;
And since with patriot zeal thou burnest,
With thee I'll live—or hang *in earnest.*

No. XVIII.

March 12.

We are indebted for the following exquisite Imitation of one
of the most beautiful Odes of Horace, to an unknown hand.
All that we can say is, that it came to us in a blank cover,
sealed with a Ducal Coronet, and that it appears evidently
to be the production of a mind not more classical than con-
vivial.

ODE.

WHITHER, O Bacchus, in thy train,*
Dost thou transport thy votary's brain
    With sudden inspiration?
Where dost thou bid me quaff my wine,
And toast new measures to combine
    The *Great* and *Little Nation?*

Say, in what tavern I shall raise †
My nightly voice in Charley's praise,

HOR. LIB. III. CARM. 25.

DITHYRAMBUS.

 * Quo me Bacche rapis, tui
    Plenum? quæ in nemora, aut quos agor in specus,
    Velox mente novâ?
                    † Quibus
    Antris egregii Cæsaris aûdiar
    Eternum meditans decus
    Stellis inserere, et consilio Jovis?

And dream of future glories,
When F—x, with salutary sway
(Terror the *Order of the Day*)
   Shall reign o'er K—ng and Tories?

My mighty feelings must have way! *
A toast I'll give—a thing I'll say,
   As yet unsaid by any,—
" OUR SOV'REIGN LORD !"—let those who doubt
My honest meaning, hear me out—
   " HIS MAJESTY—THE MANY !"

Plain folks may be surpris'd, and stare, †
As much surpris'd as B—b Ad—r
   At Russia's wooden houses;
And Russian snows, that lie so thick ; ‡
And Russian boors § that daily kick,
   With barbarous foot, their spouses.

---

    * Dicam insigne, recens, adhuc
      Indictum ore alio.
           † Non secus in jugis
    Exsomnis stupet Evias,
    Hebrum prospiciens,
               ‡ et nive candidam
    Thracen, ac *pede barbaro*
    Lustratam *Rhodopen.*

  § There appears to have been some little mistake in the
Translator here. *Rhodope* is not, as he seems to imagine, the
name of a woman, but of a mountain, and not in *Russia.*
Possibly, however, the Translator may have been misled by
the inaccuracy of the traveller here alluded to.

What joy, when drunk, at midnight's hour,*
To stroll through Covent-Garden's bow'r,
  Its various charms exploring;
And, midst its shrubs and vacant stalls,
And proud Piazza's crumbling walls,
  Hear trulls and watchmen snoring!

Parent of wine, and gin, and beer, †
The nymphs of Billingsgate you cheer;
  Naiads robust and hearty;
As Brooks's chairmen fit to wield
Their stout oak bludgeons in the field,
  To aid our virtuous party.

Mortals! no common voice you hear! ‡
Militia Colonel, Premier Peer,
  Lieutenant of a County!
I speak high things! yet, god of wine,
For thee, I fear not to resign
  These Gifts of Royal Bounty.

---

  * Ut mihi devio
Ripas, et vacuum nemus
Mirari libet!
        † O Naiadum potens
Baccharumque valentium
Proceras manibus vertere fraxinos.
  ‡ Nil parvum, aut humili modo,
  Nil mortale loquar.   Dulce periculum est
O Lenæe sequi deum
Cingentem viridi tempora pampino.

No. XIX.

March 19.

For the authenticity of the inclosed Ballad, we refer our
Readers to a Volume of MS. Poems discovered upon the
removal of some papers, during the late alterations which
have taken place at the Tax-Office, in consequence of the
Reports of the Finance Committee.

It has been communicated to our Printer by an ingenious
Friend of his, who occasionally acts for the Deputy Col-
lector of the Parish of St. Martin in the Fields ; but with-
out date, or any other mark, by which we are enabled to
guess at the particular subject of the Composition.

CHEVY CHASE.

God prosper long our Noble King,
    Our lives and safeties all :
A woeful story late there did
    In Britain's Isle befall.

D—ke Sm—ths—n, of N—rth—mb—rl—nd,
    A vow to God did make ;
The choicest gifts in fair England,
    For him and his to take.

" Stand fast, my merry men all," he cried,
  " By M—ra's Earl and me,
" And we will gain place, wealth, and pow'r
  " As Arm'd Neutrality.

" Excise and Customs, Church and Law,
  " I've begg'd from *Master Rose*;
" The Garter too—but still *the Blues*
  " I'll have, or I'll oppose."

" Now God be with him," quoth the King,
  " Sith 'twill no better be;
" I trust we have within our realm
  " Five hundred good as he."

The Duke then join'd with Charley F—x,
  A leader ware and tried,
And Ersk—ne, Sh—r—d—n, and Gr—y
  Fought stoutly by his side.

Throughout our English Parliament,
  They dealt full many a wound;
But in his King's and Country's cause,
  Pitt firmly stood his ground.

And soon a law, like arrow keen,
  Or spear, or curtal-axe,
Struck poor D—ke Sm—ths—n to the heart,
  In shape of *Powder tax*.

Sore leaning on his crutch, he cried,
   " Crop, crop, my merry men all ;
" No guinea for your heads I'll pay,
   " Though Church and State should fall."

Again the Taxing-man appear'd—
   No deadlier foe could be ;
A schedule of a cloth-yard long,
   Within his hand bore he.

" Yield thee, D—ke Sm—ths—n, and behold
   " The Assessment thou must pay ;
" Dogs, horses, houses, coaches, clocks,
   " And servants in array."

" Nay," quoth the Duke, " in thy black scroll
   " Deductions I espye—
" For those who, poor, and mean, and low,
   " With children burthen'd lie.

" And though full Sixty Thousand Pounds
   " My vassals pay to me,
" From Cornwall to *Northumberland*,
   " Through many a fair countée ;

" Yet England's Church, its King, its Laws,
   " Its cause I value not,
" Compar'd with this, my constant text,
   " *A penny sav'd, is got.*

" No drop of Princely P—rcy's blood
  " Through these cold veins doth run ;
" With Hotspur's castles, blazon, name,
  " I still am *poor* Sm—ths—n.

" Let England's youth unite in arms,
  " And every liberal hand
" With honest zeal subscribe their mite,
  " To save their native land :

" I at St. Martin's Vestry Board,
  " To swear shall be content,
" That I have children eight, and claim
  " *Deductions, Ten per Cent.*"

God bless us all from factious Foes,
  And French Fraternal Kiss ;
And grant the King may never make
  Another *Duke* like this.

No. XX.

ODE TO JACOBINISM.

I.

DAUGHTER of Hell, insatiate power,
   Destroyer of the human race,
Whose iron scourge and madd'ning hour
   Exalt the bad, the good debase;
Thy mystic force, despotic sway,
Courage and innocence dismay,
And Patriot Monarchs vainly groan
With pangs unfelt before, unpity'd and alone !

II.

When first to scourge the sons of earth,
   Thy Sire his darling Child design'd,
Gallia receiv'd the monstrous birth—
   Voltaire inform'd thy infant mind :
Well-chosen nurse ! his sophist lore
He bade thee many a year explore !
He mark'd thy progress, firm though slow,
And statesmen, princes, leagu'd with their invet'rate foe.

III.

Scar'd at thy frown terrific, fly
  The morals (antiquated brood)
Domestic Virtue, Social Joy,
  And Faith that has for ages stood;
Swift they disperse, and with them go
The Friend sincere, the gen'rous Foe.——
Traitors to God and Man avow'd,
By thee, now rais'd aloft, now crush'd beneath the
    crowd.

IV.

Revenge, in blood-stain'd robe array'd,
  Immers'd in gloomy joy profound;
Ingratitude, by guilt dismay'd,
  With anxious eye wild glancing round,
Still on thy frantic steps attend :
With Death, thy victim's only friend,
Injustice, to the truth severe,
And Anguish, dropping still the life-consuming tear.

V.

Oh swiftly on my country's head,
  Destroyer, lay thy ruthless hand;
Not yet in Gallic terrors clad,
  Nor circled by the *Marseilles Band*,
(As by th' initiate thou art seen)
With thund'ring cannon, *Guillotine*,
With screaming horrors funeral cry,
Fire, rapine, sword, and chains, and ghastly Poverty.

VI.

Thy sophist veil, dread Goddess, wear,
    Falsehood insidiously impart;
Thy philosophic train be there,
    To taint the mind, corrupt the heart;
The gen'rous Virtues of our Isle,
Teach us to hate and to revile;
Our glorious Charter's faults to scan,
Time-sanction'd Truths despise, and preach THY
    RIGHTS OF MAN.

AN ENGLISH JACOBIN.

No. XXI.

April 2.

W E premised in our Sixteenth Number, that though we should not proceed regularly with the publication of the Didactic Poem, the P ROGRESS OF M AN,—a work which, indeed, both from its bulk, and from the erudite nature of the subject, would hardly suit with the purposes of a Weekly Paper;—we should, nevertheless, give from time to time such Extracts from it, as we thought were likely to be useful to our Readers, and as were in any degree connected with the topics or events of the times.

The following Extract is from the 23d Canto of this admirable and instructive Poem;—in which the Author (whom, by a series of accidents, which we have neither the space, nor indeed the liberty, to enumerate at present, we have discovered to be Mr. H IGGINS, of *St. Mary Axe*), describes the vicious refinement of what is called Civilized Society, in respect to Marriage; contends with infinite spirit and philosophy against the factitious sacredness and indissolubility of that institution; and paints in glowing colours the happiness and utility (in a moral as well as political view) of an arrangement of an opposite sort, such as prevails in

H

countries which are yet under the influence of pure
and unsophisticated nature.

In illustration of his principles upon this subject, the
Author alludes to a popular production of the German
Drama, the title of which is the " REFORM'D HOUSE-
KEEPER," which he expresses a hope of seeing trans-
fused into the language of this country.

THE PROGRESS OF MAN.

CANTO TWENTY-THIRD.

CONTENTS.

ON MARRIAGE.

MARRIAGE *being indissoluble, the cause of its being so often unhappy.—Nature's Laws not consulted in this point.— Civilized Nations mistaken.—*OTAHEITE*—Happiness of the Natives thereof—Visited by Captain Cook, in his Majesty's Ship Endeavour—Character of Captain Cook.— Address to Circumnavigation.—Description of his Majesty's Ship Endeavour—Mast, Rigging, Sea-sickness, Prow, Poop, Mess-room, Surgeon's Mate—History of one. —Episode concerning Naval Chirurgery.—Catching a Thunny Fish.—Arrival at Otaheite.—Cast Anchor— land—Natives astonished.—Love—Liberty—Moral— Natural—Religious—Contrasted with European Manners —Strictness—Licence—Doctor's Commons—Dissolubility of* MARRIAGE *recommended—Illustrated by a Game at Cards—Whist—Cribbage—Partners changed—Why not the same in Marriage?—Illustrated by a River.—Love free.—Priests, Kings.—German Drama.—*KOTZE-BUE*'s "Housekeeper Reformed."—Moral Employments of Housekeeping described.—Hottentots sit and stare at each other—Query* WHY?*—Address to the Hottentots.—History of the Cape of Good Hope.—Resumé of the Arguments against Marriage.—Conclusion.*

PROGRESS OF MAN.

EXTRACT.

H<small>AIL</small>! beauteous lands* that crown the Southern Seas;
Dear happy seats of Liberty and Ease!
Hail! whose green coasts the peaceful ocean laves,
Incessant washing with his watery waves!
Delicious islands! to whose envied shore
Thee, gallant Cook! the ship Endeavour † bore.

There laughs the sky, there zephyr's frolic train,
And light-wing'd loves, and blameless pleasures reign:
There, when two souls congenial ties unite,
No hireling *Bonzes* chant the mystic rite;
Free every thought, each action unconfin'd,
And light those fetters which no rivets bind.

---

* The ceremony of invocation (in Didactic Poems especially) is in some measure analogous to the custom of drinking toasts: the corporeal representatives of which are always
supposed to be absent, and unconscious of the irrigation
bestowed upon their names. Hence it is, that our Author
addresses himself to the natives of an island who are not
likely to hear, and who, if they did, would not understand
him.
† His Majesty's ship Endeavour.

There in each grove, each sloping bank along,
And flow'rs and shrubs and odorous herbs among,
Each shepherd * clasp'd, with undisguis'd delight,
His yielding fair one,—in the Captain's sight;
Each yielding fair, as chance or fancy led,
Preferr'd new lovers to her sylvan bed.

Learn hence, each nymph, whose free aspiring
    mind
Europe's cold laws,† and colder customs‡ bind—
O! learn, what Nature's genial laws decree—
What Otaheite § is, let Britain be!

    *   *   *

* In justice to our Author we must observe, that there is
a delicacy in this picture, which the words, in their common
acceptation, do not convey. The amours of an English shepherd would probably be preparatory to marriage (which is
contrary to our Author's principles), or they might disgust
us by the vulgarity of their object. But in Otaheite, where
the place of shepherd is a perfect sinecure (there being no
sheep on the island) the mind of the reader is not offended
by any disagreeable allusion.

† Laws made by Parliaments, or Kings.

‡ Customs voted or imposed by ditto, not the customs
here alluded to.

§ M. Bailly and other astronomers, have observed, that
in consequence of the varying obliquity of the Ecliptic, the
climates of the circumpolar and tropical climates may, in
process of time, be materially changed. Perhaps it is not
very likely that even by these means Britain may ever become a small island in the South Seas. But this is not the
meaning of the verse—the similarity here proposed, relates
to manners, not to local situation.

Of WHIST or CRIBBAGE mark th' amusing game—
The Partners *changing*, but the SPORT the *same*.
Else would the Gamester's anxious ardour cool,
Dull every deal, and stagnant every pool.
—Yet must *one* * Man, with one unceasing Wife,
Play the LONG RUBBER of connubial life.

Yes! human laws, and laws esteem'd divine,
The generous passion straiten and confine ;
And, as a stream, when art constrains its course,
Pours its fierce torrent with augmented force,
So, Passion † narrow'd to one channel small,
Unlike the former, does not flow at all.
—For Love *then* only flaps his purple wings,
When uncontroll'd by Priestcraft or by Kings.

Such the strict rules that, in these barbarous climes,
Choke youth's fair flow'rs, and feelings turn to crimes:
And people every walk of polish'd life, ‡
With that two-headed monster, MAN and WIFE.

---

* The word *one* here, means all the inhabitants of Europe
(excepting the French, who have remedied this inconvenience), not any particular individual. The Author begs leave
to disclaim every allusion that can be construed as per-
sonal.

† As a stream—simile of dissimilitude, a mode of illustration familiar to the ancients.

‡ Walks of polished life, see " Kensington Gardens," a
poem.

Yet bright examples sometimes we observe,
Which from the general practice seem to swerve;
Such as, presented to Germania's * view,
A Kotzbue's bold emphatic pencil drew;
Such as, translated in some future age,
Shall add new glories to the British stage;
—While the moved audience sit in dumb despair,
" Like Hottentots, † *and at each other stare.*"

With look sedate, and staid beyond her years,
In matron weeds a *Housekeeper* appears.
The jingling keys her comely girdle deck—
Her 'kerchief colour'd, and her apron *check.*
Can that be Adelaide, that " soul of whim,"
Reform'd in practice, and in manner prim?
—On household cares intent, ‡ with many a sigh
She turns the pancake, and she moulds the pie;
Melts into sauces rich the savoury ham;
From the crush'd berry strains the lucid jam;

---

* Germania—Germany; a country in Europe, peopled
by the Germani; alluded to in Cæsar's Commentaries, page
1. Vol. 2. edit. prin.—See also several Didactic Poems.

† A beautiful figure of German literature. The Hottentots remarkable for staring at each other—God knows
why.

‡ This delightful and instructive picture of domestic life,
is recommended to all keepers of Boarding Schools, and
other seminaries of the same nature.

Bids brandied cherries,* by infusion slow,
Imbibe new flavour, and their own forego,
Sole cordial of her heart, sole solace of her woe!
While still, responsive to each mournful moan,
The saucepan simmers in a softer tone.

     *   *   *   *   *

---

* It is a singular quality of brandied cherries, that they
exchange their flavour for that of the liquor in which they
are immersed.—*See Knight's Progress of Civil Society.*

No. XXII.

April 9.

TO THE EDITOR

OF THE ANTI-JACOBIN.

SIR,

I saw, with strong approbation, your Specimen of ancient Sapphic Measure in English, which I think far surpasses all that Abraham Fraunce, Richard Stanyhurst, or Sir Philip Sidney himself, have produced in that style—I mean, of course, your sublime and beautiful Knife-Grinder, of which it is not too high an encomium to say, that it even rivals the efforts of the fine-ear'd Democratic Poet, Mr. Southey. But you seem not to be aware, that we have a genuine Sapphic Measure belonging to our own language, of which I now send you a short specimen.

THE JACOBIN.

I AM a hearty Jacobin,
Who own no God, and dread no sin,
Ready to dash through thick and thin
      For Freedom:

And when the Teachers of Chalk-Farm
Gave Ministers so much alarm,
And preach'd that Kings did only harm,
          I fee'd 'em.

By Bedford's cut I've trimm'd my locks,
And coal-black is my knowledge-box,
Callous to all, except hard knocks
          Of thumpers;

My eye a noble fierceness boasts,
My voice as hollow as a ghost's,
My throat oft wash'd by Factious Toasts
          In bumpers.

Whatever is in France, is right;
Terror and blood are my delight;
Parties with us do not excite
          Enough rage.

Our boasted Laws I hate and curse,
Bad from the first, by age grown worse,
I pant and sigh for univers-*
          al suffrage.

---

* This division of the word, is in the true spirit of the
English as well as the ancient Sapphic.—See the Counter-
scuffle, Counter-rat, and other Poems in this style.

Wakefield I love—adore Horne Tooke,
With pride on Jones and Thelwall look,
And hope that they, by hook or crook,
                Will prosper.

But they deserve the worst of ills,
And all the' abuse of all our quills,
Who form'd of strong and *gagging Bills*
             A cross pair.

Extinct since then each Speaker's fire,
And silent ev'ry daring lyre,*
Dum-founded they whom I would hire
             To lecture.

Tied up, alas! is every tongue
On which conviction nightly hung, †
And Thelwall looks, though yet but young,
             A spectre.
                      B. O. B.

   * There is a doubt, whether this word should not have been written *Liar*.
   † These words, of *conviction* and *hanging*, have so ominous a sound, it is rather odd they were chosen.

No. XXIII.

April 16.

W E cannot better explain to our Readers, the design of the Poem from which the following Extracts are taken, than by borrowing the expressions of the Author, Mr. HIGGINS, of *St. Mary Axe*, in the letter which accompanied the manuscript.

We must premise, that we had found ourselves called upon to remonstrate with Mr. H. on the freedom of some of the positions laid down in his other Didactic Poem, the PROGRESS of MAN ; and had in the course of our remonstrance, hinted something to the disadvantage of the *new principles* which are now afloat in the world ; and which are, in our opinion, working so much prejudice to the happiness of mankind. To this, Mr. H. takes occasion to reply—

" What you call the *new principles*, are, in fact, no-
" thing less than *new*. They are the principles of
" primeval nature, the system of original and unadul-
" terated man.

" If you mean by my addiction to *new principles*, that
" the object which I have in view in my larger Work
" (meaning the PROGRESS OF MAN) and in the se-
" veral other *concomitant* and *subsidiary* Didactic Poems
" which are necessary to complete my plan, is to re-
" store this first, and pure simplicity ; to rescue and

" recover the interesting nakedness of human nature,
" by ridding her of the cumbrous establishments which
" the folly, and pride, and self-interest of the worst
" part of our species have heaped upon her;—you are
" right.—Such is my object. I do not disavow it. Nor
" is it mine alone. There are abundance of abler hands
" at work upon it. *Encyclopedias, Treatises, Novels, Ma-*
" *gazines, Reviews*, and *New Annual Registers*, have, as
" you are well aware, done their part with activity,
" and with effect. It remained to bring the *heavy* ar-
" tillery of a Didactic Poem to bear upon the same
" object.

" If I have selected your Paper as the channel for
" conveying my labours to the Public, it was not be-
" cause I was unaware of the hostility of your princi-
" ples to mine, of the bigotry of your attachment to
" ' things as they are :'—but because, I will fairly own,
" I found some sort of cover and disguise necessary for
" securing the favourable reception of my sentiments ;
" the usual pretexts of humanity, and philanthropy,
" and fine feeling, by which we have for some time ob-
" tained a passport to the hearts and understandings
" of men, being now worn out, or exploded. I could
" not choose but smile at my success in the first instance
" in inducing *you* to adopt my Poem as your own.

" But you have called for an explanation of these
" principles of ours, and you have a right to obtain it.
" Our first principle is, then—the reverse of the trite
" and dull maxim of Pope—" *Whatever is, is right.*"
" We contend, that " *Whatever is, is wrong :*"—that

" Institutions civil and religious, that Social Order, (as
" it is called in *your* cant) and regular Government, and
" Law, and I know not what other fantastic inventions,
" are but so many cramps and fetters on the free agency
" of man's *natural intellect* and *moral sensibility*; so
" many badges of his degradation from the primal
" purity and excellence of his nature.

" Our second principle is the " *eternal and absolute*
" *Perfectibility of Man.*" We contend, that if, as is
" demonstrable, we have risen from a level with the
" *cabbages of the field* to our present comparatively in-
" telligent and dignified state of existence, by the mere
" exertion of our own *energies*; we should, if these
" *energies* were not repressed and subdued by the ope-
" ration of prejudice, and folly, by KING-CRAFT
" and PRIEST-CRAFT, and the other evils incident
" to what is called Civilized Society, continue to exert
" and expand ourselves in a proportion infinitely
" greater than any thing of which we yet have any
" notion :—in a *ratio* hardly capable of being calcu-
" lated by any science of which we are now masters;
" but which would in time raise Man from his present
" biped state, to a rank more worthy of his endow-
" ments and aspirations; to a rank in which he
" would be, as it were, *all* MIND; would enjoy un-
" clouded perspicacity and perpetual vitality ; feed on
" *Oxygene*, and never die, but *by his own consent.*

" But though the Poem of the PROGRESS OF MAN,
" alone would be sufficient to teach this system, and
" enforce these doctrines; the whole practical effect of

" them cannot be expected to be produced, but by the
" gradual perfecting of each of the sublimer sciences;
" —at the husk and shell of which we are now nibbling,
" and at the kernel whereof, in our present state, we
" cannot hope to arrive. These several Sciences will
" be the subjects of the several *auxiliary* DIDACTIC
" POEMS which I have now in hand (one of which,
" entitled THE LOVES OF THE TRIANGLES, I here-
" with transmit to you) and for the better arrange-
" ment and execution of which, I beseech you to di-
" rect your Bookseller to furnish me with a handsome
" Chambers's Dictionary; in order that I may be ena-
" bled to go through the several articles alphabetically,
" beginning with *Abracadabra*, under the first letter,
" and going down to *Zodiac*, which is to be found
" under the last.

" I am persuaded that there is no Science, however
" abstruse, nay, no Trade or Manufacture, which may
" not be taught by a Didactic Poem. In that before
" you, an attempt is made (not unsuccessfully I hope)
" to *enlist the Imagination under the banners of Geometry.*
" *Botany* I found done to my hands. And though the
" more rigid and unbending stiffness of a mathemati-
" cal subject does not admit of the same appeals to the
" warmer passions, which naturally arise out of the
" *sexual* (or, as I have heard several worthy Gentle-
" women of my acquaintance, who delight much in the
" Poem to which I allude, term it, by a slight misno-
" mer no way difficult to be accounted for—the *sensual*)
" system of Linnæus;—yet I trust that the range and

" variety of illustration with which I have endeavoured
" to ornament and enlighten the arid truths of Euclid
" and Algebra, will be found to have smoothed the
" road of Demonstration, to have softened the rugged
" features of Elementary Propositions, and, as it were,
" to have strewed the *Asses' Bridge* with flowers."

Such is the account which Mr. HIGGINS gives of his
own undertaking, and of the motives which have led
him to it. For our parts, though we have not the same
sanguine persuasion of the *absolute perfectibility* of our
species, and are in truth liable to the imputation of
being more satisfied with *things as they are*, than Mr.
HIGGINS and his Associates ;—yet, as we are in at least
the same proportion, less convinced of the practical influence of Didactic Poems, we apprehend little danger
to our Readers' morals, from laying before them Mr.
HIGGINS's doctrine in its most fascinating shape. The
Poem abounds, indeed, with beauties of the most striking kind,—various and vivid imagery, bold and unsparing impersonifications ; and similitudes and illustrations brought from the most ordinary and the most
extraordinary occurrences of nature,—from history and
fable,—appealing equally to the heart and to the under-
standing, and calculated to make the subject of which
the Poem professes to treat, rather amusing than in-
telligible. We shall be agreeably surprised to hear
that it has assisted any young Student, at either University, in his Mathematical Studies.

We need hardly add, that the Plates illustrative of
this poem (the engravings of which would have been

too expensive for our publication) are to be found in
Euclid's Elements, and other books of a similar tendency.

LOVES OF THE TRIANGLES.

ARGUMENT OF THE FIRST CANTO.

*Warning to the Profane not to approach—Nymphs and Dei-
ties of Mathematical Mythology—Cyclois of a pensive turn
—Pendulums, on the contrary, playful—and why?—
Sentimental union of the Naiads and Hydrostatics—Marriage of Euclid and Algebra.—Pulley the emblem of Mechanics—Optics of a licentious disposition—distinguished
by her Telescope and Green Spectacles.—Hyde Park Gate
on a Sunday morning—Cockneys—Coaches.—Didactic
Poetry—Nonsensia—Love delights in Angles or Corners
—Theory of Fluxions explained—Trochais, the Nymph
of the Wheel—Smoke-Jack described—Personification of
elementary or culinary Fire.—Little Jack Horner—Story
of Cinderella—Rectangle, a Magician, educated by Plato
and Menecmus—in love with Three Curves, at the same
time—served by Gins, or Genii—transforms himself into
a Cone—The Three Curves requite his Passion—description of them— Parabola, Hyperbola, and Ellipsis—Asymptotes—Conjugated Axes.—Illustrations—Rewbell, Barras,
and Lepaux, the Three virtuous Directors—Macbeth and
the Three Witches—The Three Fates—The Three Graces*

I

*—King Lear and his Three Daughters—Derby Diligence
—Catherine Wheel.—Catastrophe of Mr. Gingham, with
his Wife and Three Daughters overturned in a One-Horse
Chaise—Dislocation and Contusion two kindred Fiends—
Mail Coaches—Exhortation to Drivers to be careful—
Genius of the Post Office—Invention of Letters—Digamma
—Double Letters—remarkable Direction of one—Hippona
the Goddess of Hack-horses — Parameter and Abscissa
unite to overpower the Ordinate, who retreats down the
Axis Major, and forms himself in a Square—Isosceles, a
Giant—Dr. Rhomboides—Fifth Proposition, or Asses
Bridge—Bridge of Lodi—Buonaparte—Raft and Wind-
mills—Exhortation to the recovery of our Freedom—Con-
clusion.*

THE LOVES OF THE TRIANGLES.

A MATHEMATICAL AND PHILOSOPHICAL POEM.

INSCRIBED TO DR. DARWIN.

CANTO I.

Stay your rude steps, or e'er your feet invade
The Muses' haunts, ye Sons of War and Trade!
Nor you, ye Legion Fiends of Church and Law,
Pollute these pages with unhallow'd paw!

Ver. 1—4. Imitated from the introductory couplet to the
Economy of Vegetation.
   " Stay your rude steps, whose throbbing breasts infold
   " The Legion Fiends of Glory and of Gold."
This sentiment is here expanded into four lines.

Debas'd, corrupted, groveling, and confin'd,   5
No DEFINITIONS touch *your* senseless mind;
To *you* no POSTULATES prefer their claim,
No ardent AXIOMS *your* dull souls inflame;
For *you*, no TANGENTS touch, no ANGLES meet,
No CIRCLES join in osculation sweet!   10

For *me*, ye CISSOIDS, round my temples bend
Your wandering Curves; ye CONCHOIDS extend;
Let playful PENDULES quick vibration feel,
While silent CYCLOIS rests upon her wheel;

Ver. 6. *Definition*—A distinct notion explaining the Ge-
nesis of a thing—*Wolfius.*
Ver. 7. *Postulate*—A self-evident proposition.
Ver. 8. *Axiom*—An indemonstrable truth.
Ver. 9. *Tangents*—So called from touching, because they
touch Circles, and never cut them.
Ver. 10.—*Circles*—See Chambers's Dictionary, Article
Circle.
Ditto. *Osculation*—For the *Osculation*, or kissing of Circles
and other Curves, see Huygens, who has veiled this delicate
and inflammatory subject in the decent obscurity of a learned
language.
Ver. 11. *Cissois*—A Curve supposed to resemble the sprig
of ivy, from which it has its name, and therefore peculiarly
adapted to poetry.
Ver. 12. *Conchois*, or *Conchylis*—a most beautiful and picturesque Curve; it bears a fanciful resemblance to a *Conch*
shell. The Conchois is capable of infinite extension, and
presents a striking analogy between the Animal and Mathematical Creation. Every individual of this species, containing within itself a series of *young* Conchoids for several generations, in the same manner as the Aphides, and other
insect tribes, are observed to do

Let HYDROSTATICS, simpering as they go,   15
Lead the light Naiads on fantastic toe;
Let shrill ACOUSTICS tune the tiny lyre;
With EUCLID sage fair ALGEBRA conspire;
The' obedient pulley strong MECHANICS ply,
And wanton OPTICS roll the melting eye!   20

I see the fair fantastic forms appear,
The flaunting drapery, and the languid leer;
Fair Sylphish forms—who, tall, erect, and slim,
Dart the keen glance, and stretch the length of limb;
To viewless harpings weave the meanless dance,   25
Wave the gay wreath, and titter as they prance.

Such rich confusion charms the ravish'd sight,
When vernal Sabbaths to the Park invite.

Ver. 15. *Hydrostatics*—Water has been supposed, by several of our philosophers, to be capable of the passion of Love.
—Some later experiments appear to favour this idea—Water,
when pressed by a moderate degree of heat, has been observed to *simper*, or *simmer* (as it is more usually called.)—
The same does not hold true of any other element.

Ver. 17. *Acoustics*—The doctrine or theory of sound.

Ver. 18. *Euclid and Algebra*—The loves and nuptials of
these two interesting personages, forming a considerable
Episode in the Third Canto, are purposely omitted here.

Ver. 19. *Pulley*—So called from our Saxon word to PULL,
signifying to pull or draw.

Ver. 23. *Fair Sylphish Forms*—Vide modern prints of
nymphs and shepherds dancing to nothing at all.

Ver. 27. *Such rich confusion*—Imitated from the following

Mounts the thick dust, the coaches crowd along,
Presses round Grosvenor Gate the' impatient throng;
White-muslin'd misses and mammas are seen,   31
Link'd with gay Cockneys, glittering o'er the green:
The rising breeze unnumber'd charms displays,
And the tight ancle strikes the' astonish'd gaze.

But chief, thou Nurse of the Didactic Muse,   35
Divine NONSENSIA, all thy soul infuse;
The charms of *Secants* and of *Tangents* tell,
How Loves and Graces in an *Angle* dwell;
How slow progressive *Points* protract the *Line*,
As pendant spiders spin the filmy twine;   40

genteel and sprightly lines in the First Canto of the LOVES
OF THE PLANTS:
  So bright its folding canopy withdrawn,
  Glides the gilt landau o'er the velvet lawn,
  Of beaux and belles displays the glittering throng,
  And soft airs fan them as they glide along.
  Ver. 38. *Angle*—Gratus puellæ risus ab Angulo.—*Hor.*
  Ver. 39. *How slow progressive Points*—The Author has re-
served the picturesque imagery which the *Theory of Fluxions*
naturally suggested for his ALGEBRAIC GARDEN; where the
Fluents are described as rolling with an even current be-
tween a margin of *Curves* of the higher order, over a pebbly
channel, inlaid with *Differential Calculi.*
  In the following six lines he has confined himself to a
strict explanation of the Theory, according to which Lines
are supposed to be generated by the motion of Points;—Planes
by the lateral motion of Lines;—and Solids from Planes, by
a similar process.
  Quære—Whether a practical application of this Theory
would not enable us to account for the Genesis, or original

How lengthen'd *Lines*, impetuous sweeping round,
Spread the wide *Plane*, and mark its circling bound ;

formation of Space itself, in the same manner in which Dr.
Darwin has traced the whole of the organized creation to
his Six Filaments—Vide ZOONOMIA.   We may conceive
the whole of our present Universe to have been originally
concentered in a single Point—We may conceive this Primeval Point, or *Punctum Saliens* of the Universe, evolving
itself by its own energies, to have moved forwards in
a right Line, *ad infinitum*, till it grew tired—After which,
the right Line, which it had generated would begin to put
itself in motion in a lateral direction, describing an Area of
infinite extent.   This Area, as soon as it became conscious
of its own existence, would begin to ascend or descend, according as its specific gravity might determine it, forming
an immense solid space filled with Vacuum, and capable of
containing the present existing Universe.

Space being thus obtained, and presenting a suitable Ni-
dus, or receptacle for the generation of Chaotic Matter, an
immense deposit of it would gradually be accumulated :—
After which, the Filament of *Fire* being produced in the
Chaotic Mass, by an *Idiosyncracy*, or self-formed habit analogous to fermentation, *Explosion* would take place; *Suns*
would be shot from the Central Chaos ;—*Planets* from *Suns*;
and *Satellites* from *Planets*.   In this state of things, the Filament of *Organization* would begin to exert itself, in those in-
dependent masses which, in proportion to their bulk, exposed the greatest surface to the action of *Light* and *Heat.*
This Filament, after an infinite series of ages, would begin
to *ramify*, and its viviparous offspring would diversify their
forms and habits, so as to accommodate themselves to the
various *incunabula* which Nature had prepared for them.—
Upon this view of things, it seems highly probable that the
first effort of Nature terminated in the production of Vege-
tables, and that these being abandoned to their own *energies*,
by degrees detached themselves from the surface of the earth,
and supplied themselves with wings or feet, according as
their different propensities determined them, in favour of

How *Planes*, their substance with their motion grown,
Form the huge *Cube*, the *Cylinder*, the *Cone*.

Lo! where the chimney's sooty tube ascends,   45
The fair TROCHAIS from the corner bends!
Her coal-black eyes upturn'd, incessant mark
The eddying smoke, quick flame, and volant spark;
Mark with quick ken, where flashing in between
Her much loved *Smoke-Jack* glimmers thro' the scene;
Mark, how his various parts together tend,   51
Point to one purpose,—in one object end:
The spiral *grooves* in smooth meanders flow,   ⎫
Drags the long *chain*, the polish'd axles glow,   ⎬
While slowly circumvolves the piece of beef below: ⎭
The conscious fire with bickering radiance burns,   56
Eyes the rich joint, and roasts it as it turns.

aerial and terrestrial existence.   Others by an inherent disposition to society and civilization, and by a stronger effort
of *volition*, would become Men.   These, in time, would re-
strict themselves to the use of their *hind feet*: their *tails*
would gradually rub off, by sitting in their caves or huts,
as soon as they arrived at a domesticated state: they would
invent *language*, and the use of *fire*, with our present and
hitherto imperfect system of *Society*. In the mean while, the
Fuci and *Algæ*, with the *Corallines* and *Madrepores*, would
transform themselves into *fish*, and would gradually popu-
late all the sub-marine portion of the globe.

Ver. 46. *Trochais*—The Nymph of the Wheel, supposed
to be in love with Smoke-Jack.

Ver. 56. *The Conscious Fire*—The Sylphs and Genii of the
different Elements have a variety of innocent occupations
assigned them: those of fire are supposed to divert them-

So youthful Horner roll'd the roguish eye,
Cull'd the dark plum from out his Christmas pye,
And cried, in self-applause—" How good a boy
    am I."   60

So she, sad victim of domestic spite,
Fair Cinderella, past the wintry night,
In the lone chimney's darksome nook immur'd,
Her form disfigur'd, and her charms obscur'd.
Sudden her God-mother appears in sight,   65
Lifts the charm'd rod, and chants the mystic rite.
The chanted rite the maid attentive hears,
And feels new ear-rings deck her listening ears;
While 'midst her towering tresses, aptly set,
Shines bright, with quivering glance, the smart aigrette;
Brocaded silks the splendid dress complete,   71
And the Glass Slipper grasps her fairy feet.

selves with writing *Kunkel* in phosphorus.—*See* ECONOMY OF
VEGETATION.

   " Or mark, with shining letters Kunkel's name
   " In the slow *phosphor's* self-consuming flame."
   Ver. 68. *Listening ears*—Listening, and therefore peculiarly suited to a pair of diamond ear-rings. See the description of Nebuchadnezzar, in his transformed state.
   Nor flattery's self can pierce his *pendant ears.*
In poetical diction, a person is said to ' *breathe the* BLUE
air,' and to ' *drink the* HOARSE *wave!*'—not that the colour
of the sky, or the noise of the water, has any reference to
drinking or breathing, but because the Poet obtains the advantage of thus describing his subject under a *double relation,*
in the same manner in which material objects present themselves to our different senses at the same time.

Six cock-tail'd mice transport her to the ball,
And liveried lizards wait upon her call.

Alas! that partial Science should approve   75
The sly RECTANGLE's too licentious love!
For *three* bright nymphs, &c. &c.

(To be continued.)

Ver. 73. *Cock-tail'd Mice*—coctilibus Muris. *Ovid.*—There
is reason to believe, that the *murine*, or *mouse* species, were
anciently much more numerous than at the present day. It
appears from the sequel of the line, that Semiramis surround-
ed the city of Babylon with a number of these animals.

Dicitur altam
Coctilibus Muris cinxisse Semiramis urbem.

It is not easy at present to form any conjecture with respect to the end, whether of ornament or defence, which
they could be supposed to answer. I should be inclined to
believe, that in this instance the mice were dead, and that so
vast a collection of them must have been furnished by way
of tribute, to free the country from these destructive animals. This superabundance of the *murine* race, must have
been owing to their immense fecundity, and to the comparatively tardy reproduction of the *feline* species. The traces
of this disproportion are to be found in the early history of
every country.—The ancient laws of Wales estimate a Cat
at the price of as much corn as would be sufficient to cover
her, if she were suspended by the tail with her fore-feet
touching the ground.—See Howel Dha.—In Germany, it is
recorded that an army of rats, a larger animal of the *mus*
tribe, were employed as the Ministers of Divine vengeance
against a feudal Tyrant; and the commercial legend of our
own Whittington, might probably be traced to an equally
authentic origin.

No. XXIV.

April 23.

THE LOVES OF THE TRIANGLES.

A MATHEMATICAL AND PHILOSOPHICAL POEM.

[*Continued.*]

CANTO I.

A LAS ! that partial Science should approve   75
The sly RECTANGLE's too licentious love !
For *three* bright nymphs the wily wizard burns ;—
Three bright-ey'd nymphs requite his flame by turns.
Strange force of magic skill ! combin'd of yore
With Plato's science and Menecmus' lore.   80

Ver. 76. *Rectangle*—"A figure which has one Angle, or more, of ninety degrees." Johnson's Dictionary.—It here means a right-angled Triangle, which is therefore incapable of having more than one Angle of ninety degrees, but which may, according to our Author's *Prosopopœia*, be supposed to be in love with Three, or any greater number of nymphs.

Ver. 80. *Plato's and Menecmus' lore*—Proclus attributes the discovery of the Conic Sections to Plato, but obscurely. Eratosthenes seems to adjudge it to Menecmus. "*Neque Menecmeos necesse erit in Cono secare ternarios.*" (Vide *Montucla*.) From Greece they were carried to Alexandria, where (ac-

In *Afric*'s schools, amid those sultry sands
High on its base where Pompey's pillar stands,
This learnt the Seer; and learnt, alas! too well,
Each scribbled talisman, and smoky spell:
What mutter'd charms, what soul-subduing arts   85
Fell Zatanai to his sons imparts.

    GINS—black and huge! who in Dom-Daniel's cave
Writhe your scorch'd limbs on sulphur's azure wave,
Or, shivering, yell amidst eternal snows,
Where cloud-cap'd Caf protrudes his granite toes; 90

cording to our Author's beautiful fiction) *Rectangle* either
did or might learn magic.
    Ver. 86. *Zatanai*—Supposed to be the same with Satan.—
Vide the *New Arabian Nights*, translated by Cazotte, author
of "*Le Diable amoureux.*"
    Ver. 87. *Gins*—the Eastern name for Genii.—Vide Tales
of ditto.
    Ver. 87. *Dom-Daniel*—a sub-marine palace near Tunis,
where Zatanai usually held his court.—Vide *New Arabian
Nights.*
    Ver. 88. *Sulphur*—A substance which, when cold, reflects
the yellow rays, and is therefore said to be yellow. When
raised to a temperature at which it *attracts oxygene* (a process
usually called *burning*), it emits a blue flame. This may be
beautifully exemplified, and at a moderate expence, by ig-
niting those *fasciculi* of brimstone *matches*, frequently sold (so
frequently, indeed, as to form one of the London cries) by
women of an advanced age, in this metropolis. They will
be found to yield an *azure*, or blue light.
    Ver. 90. *Caf*—the Indian *Caucasus.*—Vide Bailly's *Lettres
sur l'Atlantide*, in which he proves that this was the native
country of Gog and Magog (now resident in Guildhall), as
well as of the Peris, or fairies, of the Asiatic Romances.

(Bound by his will, *Judæa's* fabled king,
Lord of *Aladdin's* Lamp and mystic Ring.)
Gins! ye remember!—for your toil convey'd
Whate'er of drugs the powerful charm could aid;
Air, earth, and sea ye search'd, and where below   95
Flame embryo lavas, young volcanoes glow,—
Gins! ye beheld appall'd the enchanter's hand
Wave in dark air the' *Hypothenusal* wand;
Saw him the mystic *Circle* trace, and wheel
With head erect, and far extended heel;   100

Ver. 91. *Judæa's fabled king*—Mr. HIGGINS does not
mean to deny that Solomon was really King of Judæa. The
epithet *fabled*, applies to that empire over the Genii, which
the retrospective generosity of the Arabian fabulists has bestowed upon this monarch.

Ver. 96. *Young volcanoes*—The genesis of burning mountains was never, till lately, well explained. Those with
which we are best acquainted, are certainly not viviparous;
it is therefore probable, that there exists, in the centre of the
earth, a considerable reservoir of their eggs, which, during
the obstetrical convulsions of general earthquakes, produce
new volcanoes.

Ver. 100. *Far extended heel*—The personification of *Rectangle*, besides answering a poetical purpose, was necessary
to illustrate Mr. HIGGINS's philosophical opinions. The
ancient mathematicians conceived that a Cone was generated
by the revolution of a Triangle; but this, as our Author
justly observes, would be impossible, without supposing in
the Triangle that *expansive nisus*, discovered by Blumen-
bach, and improved by Darwin, which is peculiar to animated matter, and which alone explains the whole mystery
of organization. Our enchanter sits on the ground, with his
heels stretched out, his head erect, his wand (or *Hypothenuse*)
resting on the extremities of his feet and the tip of his nose

Saw him, with speed that mock'd the dazzled eye,
Self-whirl'd, in quick gyrations eddying fly :
Till done the potent spell—behold him grown
Fair *Venus'* emblem—the *Phœnician* CONE.

Triumphs the Seer, and now secure observes   105
The kindling passions of the *rival* CURVES.

And first, the fair PARABOLA behold,
Her timid arms, with virgin blush, unfold!
Though, on one *focus* fix'd, her eyes betray
A heart that glows with love's resistless sway,   110
Though, climbing oft, she strive with bolder grace
Round his tall neck to clasp her fond embrace,

(as is finely expressed in the engraving in the original work)
and revolves upon his bottom with great velocity. His skin,
by magical means, has acquired an indefinite power of expansion, as well as that of assimilating to itself all the *azote*
of the air, which he decomposes by expiration from his lungs
—an immense quantity, and which, in our present unimpro-
ved and uneconomical mode of breathing, is quite thrown
away.   By this simple process the transformation is very naturally accounted for.

Ver. 104. *Phœnician Cone*—It was under this shape that Venus was worshipped in Phœnicia.   Mr. HIGGINS thinks it
was the *Venus Urania*, or Celestial Venus; in allusion to
which, the Phœnician grocers first introduced the practice
of preserving sugar loaves in blue or sky-coloured paper—
he also believes that the *conical* form of the original grenadiers' caps was typical of the loves of Mars and Venus.

Ver. 107. *Parabola*—The curve described by projectiles
of all sorts, as bombs, shuttle-cocks, &c.

Still e'er she reach it, from his polish'd side
Her trembling hands in devious *Tangents* glide.

Not thus HYPERBOLA :—with subtlest art   115
The blue-eyed wanton plays her changeful part ;
Quick as her *conjugated axes* move
Through every posture of luxurious love,
Her sportive limbs with easiest grace expand ;
Her charms unveil'd provoke the lover's hand :— 120
Unveil'd, except in many a filmy ray
Where light *Asymptotes* o'er her bosom play,
Nor touch her glowing skin, nor intercept the
    day.

Yet why, ELLIPSIS, at thy fate repine ?
More lasting bliss, securer joys are thine.   125
Though to each fair his treacherous wish may stray,
Though each, in turn, may seize a transient sway,
'Tis thine with mild coercion to restrain,
Twine round his struggling heart, and bind with end-
    less chain.

Ver. 115. *Hyperbola*—Not figuratively speaking, as in rhe-
toric, but mathematically ; and therefore blue-eyed.
Ver. 122. *Asymptotes*—" Lines which though they may
approach still nearer together, till they are nearer than the
least assignable distance, yet being still produced infinitely,
will never meet."—Johnson's Dictionary.
Ver. 124. *Ellipsis*—A curve, the revolution of which on
its axis produces an Ellipsoid, or solid resembling the eggs
of birds, particularly those of the gallinaceous tribe. *Ellipsis* is the only curve that embraces the Cone.

Thus, happy France! in thy regenerate land,   130
Where TASTE with RAPINE saunters hand in
     hand ;
Where, nurs'd in seats of innocence and bliss,
REFORM greets TERROR with fraternal kiss ;
Where mild PHILOSOPHY first taught to scan
The *wrongs* of PROVIDENCE, and *rights* of MAN ; 135
Where MEMORY broods o'er FREEDOM's earlier
     scene,
The *Lanthern* bright, and brighter *Guillotine* ;—
Three gentle swains evolve their longing arms,
And woo the young REPUBLIC's virgin charms :
And though proud *Barras* with the fair succeed,   140
Though not in vain the' Attorney *Rewbell* plead,
Oft doth the' impartial nymph their love forego,
To clasp thy crooked shoulders, blest *Lepaux!*

So, with dark dirge athwart the blasted heath,
Three Sister Witches hail'd the' appall'd Macbeth. 145

So, the *Three* Fates beneath grim Pluto's roof,
Strain the dun warp, and weave the murky woof;
'Till deadly Atropos with fatal sheers
Slits the thin promise of the' expected years,
While 'midst the dungeon's gloom or battle's din, 150
Ambition's victims perish, as they spin.

Thus, the *Three* Graces on the Idalian green,
Bow with deft homage to Cythera's Queen ;

Her polish'd arms with pearly bracelets deck,
Part her light locks, and bare her ivory neck;   155
Round her fair form etherial odours throw,
And teach the' unconscious zephyrs where to blow.
Floats the thin gauze, and glittering as they play,
The bright folds flutter in phlogistic day.

So, with his Daughters *Three*, the' unscepter'd Lear
Heav'd the loud sigh, and pour'd the glistering tear;
His Daughters *Three*, save one alone, conspire
(Rich in his gifts) to spurn their generous Sire;
Bid the rude storm his hoary tresses drench,
Stint the spare meal, the Hundred Knights retrench;
Mock his mad sorrow, and with alter'd mien   166
Renounce the daughter, and assert the queen.
A father's griefs his feeble frame convulse,
Rack his white head, and fire his feverous pulse;
Till kind Cordelia soothes his soul to rest,   170
And folds the Parent-Monarch to her breast.

Thus some fair Spinster grieves in wild affright,
Vex'd with dull megrim, or vertigo light;
Pleas'd round the fair *Three* dawdling doctors stand,
Wave the white wig, and stretch the asking hand, 175
State the grave doubt,—the nauseous draught decree,
And all receive, though none deserve, a fee.

So down thy hill, romantic Ashbourn, glides
The Derby dilly, carrying *Three* INSIDES.

One in each corner sits, and lolls at ease,   180
With folded arms, propt back, and outstretch'd knees;
While the press'd *Bodkin*, punch'd and squeez'd to
    death,
Sweats in the midmost place, and scolds, and pants for
    breath.

        [*To be continued.*]

K

No. XXV.

April 30.

BRISSOT'S GHOST.

As at the Shakespeare Tavern dining,
  O'er the well replenish'd board
Patriotic Chiefs reclining,
  Quick and large libations pour'd;
While, in fancy, great and glorious,
  'Midst the Democratic storm,
Fox's Crew, with shout victorious,
  Drank to *Radical Reform.*

Sudden up the staircase sounding,
  Hideous yells and shrieks were heard;
Then, each guest with fear confounding,
  A grim train of Ghosts appear'd:
Each a head with anguish gasping,
  (Himself a trunk deform'd with gore)
In his hand, terrific, clasping,
  Stalk'd across the wine-stain'd floor.

On them gleam'd the lamp's blue lustre,
  When stern Brissot's grizly shade
His sad bands was seen to muster,
  And his bleeding troops array'd.

Through the drunken crowd he hied him,
    Where the Chieftain sate enthron'd,
There, his shadowy trunks beside him,
    Thus in threatening accents groan'd.

" Heed, oh heed our fatal story,
    " (I am Brissot's injur'd Ghost,)
" You who hope to purchase glory
    " In that field where I was lost!
" Though dread Pitt's expected ruin
    " Now your soul with triumph cheers,
" When you think on our undoing,
    " You will mix your hopes with fears.

" See these helpless headless Spectres
    " Wandering through the midnight gloom :
" Mark their Jacobinic Lectures
    " Echoing from the silent tomb.
" These, thy soul with terror filling,
    " Once were Patriots fierce and bold"—
(Each his head with gore distilling
    Shakes, the whilst his tale is told.)

" Some from that dread engine's carving
    " In vain contriv'd their heads to save—
" See Barbaroux and Petion * starving
    " In the Languedocian Cave !

* Such was the end of these Worthies. They were found
starved to death in a cave in Languedoc. *Vide Barrere's Rep.*

" See in a higgler's * hamper buckled
    " How Louvet's soaring spirit lay!
" How virtuous Roland, † hapless Cuckold,
    " Blew, what brains he had, away.

" How beneath the power of Marat
    " Condorcet, blaspheming, fell,
" Begg'd some laudanum of Garat, ‡
    " Drank ;—and slept,—to wake in hell!
" Oh that, with worthier souls uniting,
    " I in my Country's cause had shone!
" Had died my Sovereign's battle fighting,
    " Or nobly propt his sinking throne!—

* See Louvet's *Recit de mes Perils.*
† The virtuous Roland. This philosophic coxcomb is the idol of those who admire the French Revolution *up to a certain point.*
‡ This little anecdote is not generally known.—It is strikingly pathetic.—Garat has recorded this circumstance in a very eloquent sentence—" O toi qui arrêtas la main, " avec laquelle tu traçais le progrès de l'esprit humain, pour " porter sur tes levres le breuvage mortel, d'autres pensées, " et d'autres sentimens, ont incliné ta volenté vers le tom-" beau, dans ta dernière délibération.—(Garat, it seems, did " not choose to poison *himself.*)—Tu as rendu à la liberté " eternelle ton ame Républicaine par ce poison qui avait été " partagé entre nous comme le pain entre des frères."
    " Oh you, who with that hand which was tracing the pro-" gress of the human mind, approached the mortal mixture " to your lips—it was by other thoughts and other senti-" ments that your judgment was at length determined in that " last deliberated act—You restored your Republican spirit " to an eternal freedom, by that poison which we had shared " together, like a morsel of bread between two brothers."

" But hold!—I scent the gales of morning—
　" Covent-Garden's clock strikes One!
" Heed, oh heed my earnest warning,
　" Ere England is, like France, undone!
" To St. Stephen's quick repairing,
　" Your dissembled Mania end;
" And your errors past, forswearing,
　" Stand at length your Country's Friend!"

No. XXVI.

May 7.

LOVES OF THE TRIANGLES.

The frequent sollicitations which we have received for a con-
tinuation of the Loves of the Triangles, have induced us
to lay before the Public (with Mr. Higgins's permission)
the concluding lines of the Canto. The catastrophe of Mr.
and Mrs. Gingham, and the Episode of Hippona, con-
tained, in our apprehension, several reflections of too free
a nature. The Conspiracy of Parameter and Abscissa
against the Ordinate, is written in a strain of Poetry so
very splendid and dazzling, as not to suit the more tran-
quil majesty of diction which our Readers admire in Mr.
Higgins. We have therefore begun our Extract with the
Loves of the Giant Isosceles, and the Picture of the Asses
Bridge, and its several Illustrations.

CANTO I.

EXTRACT.

'Twas thine alone, O youth of giant frame,
Isosceles!* that rebel heart to tame!

---

* *Isosceles*—An equi-crural Triangle—It is represented as
a *Giant*, because Mr. HIGGINS says he has observed that
procerity is much promoted by the equal length of the legs,
more especially when they are long legs.

In vain coy Mathesis * thy presence flies :
Still turn her fond hallucinating † eyes ;
Thrills with *Galvanic* fires ‡ each tortuous nerve,
Throb her blue veins, and dies her cold reserve.
—Yet strives the fair, till in the Giant's breast
She sees the mutual passion flame confess'd :
Where'er he moves, she sees his tall limbs trace
Internal Angles § *equal at the Base* ;
Again she doubts him : but *produc'd at will,*
She sees *th' external Angles equal still.*

* *Mathesis*—The doctrine of Mathematics—Pope calls her mad *Mathesis.*—Vide *Johnson's Dictionary.*

† *Hallucinating*—The disorder with which Mathesis is affected, is a disease of *increased volition*, called *erotomania*, or *sentimental love.* It is the fourth species of the second genus of the first order and third class ; in consequence of which Mr. Hackman shot Miss Ray in the lobby of the playhouse. —Vide *Zoonomia*, Vol. II. p. 363, 365.

‡ *Galvanic Fires*—Dr. Galvani is a celebrated philosopher at Turin. He has proved that the electric fluid is the proximate cause of nervous sensibility ; and Mr. HIGGINS is of opinion, that by means of this discovery, the sphere of our disagreeable sensations may be, in future, considerably enlarged. " Since dead frogs (says he) are awakened by this "fluid, to such a degree of posthumous sensibility, as to jump "out of the glass in which they are placed, why not men, who "are sometimes so much more sensible when alive ? And if "so, why not employ this new stimulus to deter mankind "from dying (which they so pertinaciously continue to do) "of various old-fashioned diseases, notwithstanding all the "brilliant discoveries of modern philosophy, and the ex-"ample of Count Cagliostro ?"

§ *Internal Angles*, &c.—This is an exact versification of Euclid's 5th theorem.—Vide *Euclid in loco.*

Say, blest Isosceles! what favouring pow'r,
Or love, or chance, at night's auspicious hour,
While to the *Asses-Bridge* entranced you stray'd,
Led to the *Asses-Bridge* the enamour'd maid?
—The *Asses-Bridge*, for ages doom'd to hear
The deafening surge assault his wooden ear,
With joy repeats sweet sounds of mutual bliss,
The soft susurrant sigh, and gently-murmuring kiss.

So thy dark arches, *London Bridge*, bestride
Indignant Thames, and part his angry tide,
There oft—returning from those green retreats,
Where fair *Vauxhallia* decks her sylvan seats;—
Where each spruce nymph from city compters free,
Sips the froth'd syllabub, or fragrant tea;
While with sliced ham, scrap'd beef, and burnt cham-
        pagne,
Her 'prentice lover soothes his amorous pain;
—There oft, in well-trimm'd wherry, glide along
Smart beaux and giggling belles, a glittering throng;
Smells the tarr'd rope—with undulation fine
Flaps the loose sail—the silken awnings shine;

---

* *Asses-Bridge*—Pons Asinorum—The name usually given
to the before-mentioned theorem—though, as Mr. HIGGINS
thinks, absurdly. He says, that having frequently watched
companies of asses during their passage of a bridge, he never
discovered in them any symptoms of geometrical instinct
upon the occasion.—But he thinks that with Spanish asses,
which are much larger (vide *Townsend's Travels through
Spain*), the case may possibly be different.

"Shoot we the bridge!"—the venturous boatmen cry—
"Shoot we the bridge!"—the exulting fare* reply.
—Down the steep fall the headlong waters go,
Curls the white foam, the breakers roar below.
—The veering helm the dextrous steersman stops,
Shifts the thin oar, the fluttering canvas drops;
Then with clos'd eyes, clench'd hands, and quick-
        drawn breath,
Darts at the central arch, nor heeds the gulf beneath.
—Full 'gainst the pier the unsteady timbers knock,
The loose planks starting own the impetuous shock;
The shifted oar, dropt sail, and steadied helm,
With angry surge the closing waters whelm—
—Laughs the glad Thames, and clasps each fair one's
        charms
That screams and scrambles in his oozy arms.
—Drench'd each smart garb, and clogg'd each strug-
        gling limb,
Far o'er the stream the Cockneys sink or swim;
While each badg'd boatman † clinging to his oar,
Bounds o'er the buoyant wave, and climbs the ap-
        plauding shore.

So, towering Alp! from thy majestic ridge ‡
Young Freedom gaz'd on Lodi's blood-stain'd *Bridge*;

---

* *Fare*—A person, or a number of persons conveyed in a
hired vehicle by land or water.

† *Badged boatmen*—Boatmen sometimes wear a *badge*, to
distinguish them : especially those who belong to the Water-
men's Company.

‡ *Alp or Alps*—A ridge of mountains which separate the

—Saw, in thick throngs, conflicting armies rush,
Ranks close on ranks, and squadrons squadrons crush;
—Burst in bright radiance through the battle's storm,
Waved her broad hands, display'd her awful form;
Bade at her feet regenerate nations bow,
And twin'd the wreath round Buonaparte's brow.
—Quick with new lights, fresh hopes, and alter'd zeal,
The slaves of Despots dropt the blunted steel:
Exulting Victory own'd her favourite child,
And freed Liguria clapt her hands and smil'd.

Nor long the time ere Britain's shores shall greet
The warrior-sage, with gratulation sweet:
Eager to grasp the wreath of Naval Fame,
The GREAT REPUBLIC plans the *Floating Frame!*
—O'er the huge plane gigantic *Terror* stalks,
And counts with joy the close-compacted balks:
Of young-ey'd *Massacres* the Cherub crew,
Round their grim chief the mimic task pursue;
Turn the stiff screw,* apply the strengthening clamp,
Drive the long bolt, or fix the stubborn cramp,
Lash the reluctant beam, the cable splice,
Join the firm dove-tail with adjustment nice,

North of Italy from the South of Germany. They are evidently primeval and volcanic, consisting of granite, toad-
stone, and basalt, and several other substances, containing
animal and vegetable recrements, and affording numberless
undoubted proofs of the infinite antiquity of the earth, and
of the consequent falsehood of the Mosaic Chronology.

* *Turn the stiff screw,* &c.—The harmony and imagery of

O tempt the treacherous sea no more,
But gallantly regain the shore.

Scarce could our guardian Goddess, Reason,
Ensure your timbers through the season.
Though built of wood from fam'd Marseilles,
Well-mann'd from galleys, and from jails,
Though with Lepaux's, and Rewbell's aid,
By Pleville's skill your keel was laid;
Though lovely Stael, and lovelier Stone,*
Have work'd their fingers to the bone,
And cut their petticoats to rags
To make your bright Three Colour'd Flags;
Yet sacrilegious grape and ball
Deform the works of Stone and Stael,
And trembling, without food or breeches,
Our sailors curse the *painted* ————.†

    O Navis, referent in mare te novi
    Fluctus—O qui agis?—fortiter occupa
        Portum: Nonne vides, ut
        Nudum remigio latus,
    Et malus celeri saucius Africo
    Antennæque gemant? Ac sine funibus
        Vix durare carinæ
        Possint imperiosius
    Æquor? Non tibi sunt integra lintea;
    Non Dii, quos iterum pressa voces malo;
        Quamvis Pontica pinus,
        Silvæ filia nobilis,
    Jactes et genus et nomen inutile.
    Nil *pictis* timidus navita *puppibus*

* Stone—better known by the name of Williams.
† We decline printing this rhyme at length, from obvious

Children of Muskein's anxious care,
Source of my hope and my despair,
GUN-BOATS—unless you mean hereafter
To furnish food for British laughter—
Sweet GUN-BOATS, with your gallant crew,
Tempt not the rocks of SAINT MARCOU;
Beware the Badger's bloody pennant,
And that d——d invalid LIEUTENANT!

> Fidit. Tu nisi ventis
> Debes ludibrium, cave,
> Nuper sollocitum quæ mihi tædium,
> Nunc desiderium, curaque non levis,
>   Interfusa nitentes
>   Vites æquora Cycladas.

ELEGY

ON THE DEATH OF JEAN BON ST. ANDRÉ'.

The following exquisite tribute to the memory of an
unfortunate Republican, is written with such a touching sensibility, that those who can command salt tears,
must prepare to shed them. The narrative is simple,

reasons of delicacy; at the same time that it is so accurate a
translation of *pictis puppibus*, that we know not how to suppress it, without doing the utmost injustice to the general
spirit of the Poem.

and unaffected; the event in itself interesting; the moral obvious and awful.—We have only to observe, that as this account of the transaction is taken from the French papers, it may possibly be somewhat partial.—The Dey's own statement of the affair has not yet been received. Every friend of humanity will join with us, in expressing a candid and benevolent hope, that this business may not tend to kindle the flames of war between these two Unchristian Powers; but that by mutual concession and accommodation, they may come to some point (short of the restoration of Jean Bon's head on his shoulders, which in this stage of the discussion is hardly practicable), by which the peace of the Pagan world may be preserved. For our part, we pretend not to decide from which quarter the concessions ought principally to be made. It is but candid to allow that there are probably faults on *both sides,* in this, as in most other cases. For the character of the Dey, we profess a sincere respect on the one hand; and on the other, we naturally wish that the head of Jean Bon St. André should be reserved for his own Guillotine.

ELEGY: OR DIRGE.

I.

ALL in the town of Tunis,
In Africa the torrid,
On a Frenchman of rank
Was play'd such a prank,
As Lepaux must think quite horrid.

II.

No story half so shocking,
By kitchen fire or laundry,
Was ever heard tell,—
As that which befell
The great Jean Bon St. André.

III.

Poor John was a gallant Captain,
In battles much delighting;
He fled full soon
On the First of June—
But he bade the rest keep fighting.

IV.

To Paris then returning,
And recover'd from his panic,

He translated the plan
Of *Paine's Rights of Man*,
Into language Mauritanic.

V.

He went to teach at Tunis—
Where as Consul he was settled—
  Amongst other things,
   " That the people are kings !"
Whereat the Dey was nettled.

VI.

The Moors being rather stupid,
And in temper somewhat mulish,
  Understood not a word
  Of the Doctrine they heard,
And thought the Consul foolish.

VII.

He form'd a *Club* of *Brothers*,
And mov'd some resolutions—
  " Ho! Ho! (says the Dey),
  " So this is the way
" That the French make *Revolutions*."

VIII.

The Dey then gave his orders
In Arabic and Persian—
  " Let no more be said—
  " But bring me his head !—
" These *Clubs* are my aversion."

IX.

The Consul quoted Wicquefort,
And Puffendorf and Grotius;
  And prov'd from Vattel
  Exceedingly well,
Such a deed would be quite atrocious.

X.

'Twould have moved a Christian's bowels
To hear the doubts he stated;—
  But the Moors they did
  As they were bid,
And strangled him while he prated.

XI.

His head with a sharp-edg'd sabre
They sever'd from his shoulders,
  And stuck it on high,
  Where it caught the eye,
To the wonder of all beholders.

XII.

This sure is a doleful story
As e'er you heard or read of;—
  If at Tunis you prate
  Of matters of state,
Anon they cut your head off!

XIII.

But we hear the French Directors
Have thought the point so knotty;

That the Dey having shewn
He dislikes Jean Bon,
They have sent him Bernadotte.

On recurring to the French papers, to verify our
Correspondent's statement of this singular adventure
of Jean Bon St. André, we discovered, to our great
mortification, that it happened at Algiers, and not at
Tunis.—We should have corrected this mistake, but
for two reasons—first, that Algiers would not stand in
the verse; and, secondly, that we are informed by the
young man who conducts the Geographical Department of the Morning Chronicle, that both the towns
are in Africa, or Asia (he is not quite certain which),
and, what is more to the purpose, that both are peopled
by Moors. Tunis, therefore, may stand.

No. XXVIII.

May 21.

We have received the following Letter with the Poem that accompanies it, from a Gentleman whose political opinions have hitherto differed from our own ; but who appears to feel, as every man who loves his Country must, that there can be but one sentiment entertained by Englishmen at the present moment.

Were we at liberty, we should be happy to do justice to the Author, and credit to ourselves, by mentioning his name.

TO THE

EDITOR OF THE ANTI-JACOBIN.

SIR,

However men may have differed on the political or constitutional questions which have of late been brought into discussion—whatever opinions they may have held on the system or conduct of administration—there can surely be now but one sentiment as to the instant necessity of firm and strenuous union for the preservation of our very existence as a people ; and if degrees of obligation could be admitted, where the utmost is required from all, it should seem, that in this cause

the Opposers of Administration stand doubly pledged;
for, with what face of consistency can men pretend to
stickle for points of Constitutional Liberty at home,
who will not be found amongst the foremost at their
posts, to defend their Country from the yoke of Foreign Slavery?

That there should be any set of men so infatuated,
as not to be convinced that the object of the Enemy
must be the utter destruction of these countries, after
making the largest allowance for the effects of prejudice and passion, it is not easy to conceive. Such, however, we are told there are. They believe then, that
after a long series of outrage, insult, and injury, in the
height of their animosity and presumption, these moderate, mild, disinterested Conquerors will invade us
in arms, out of pure love and kindness, merely for our
good, only to make us wiser, and better, and happier,
and more prosperous than before!

Future events lie hid in the volume of Fate, but the
intentions of men may be known by almost infallible
indications. Passion and interest, the two mighty motives of human action, determine the Government of
France to attempt the abolition of the British Empire!
and if, abandoned by God and our right arm, we should
flinch in the conflict, that destruction will be opera-
tive to the full of their gigantic and monstrous imagi-
nations!—Harbours filled up with the ruins of their
towns and arsenals—the Thames rendered a vast mo-
rass, by burying the Imperial City in her bosom—but
I will not proceed in the horrible picture.

Are we then, it may be asked, to wage eternal war? —No; a glorious resistance leads to an honourable peace. The French people have been long weary of the war; their spirit has been forced by a system which must end in the failure of the engagement to give them the plunder of this Country. They will awake from their dream, and raise a cry for peace, which their government will not dare to resist. The Monarchs of Europe must now begin clearly to perceive, that their fate hangs on the destiny of England; they will unite to compel a satisfactory peace on a broad foundation; and Peace, when War has been tried to the utmost, will probably be permanent. A few years of wise economy and redoubled industry, will place us again on the rising scale; and if the pressure of the times may have rendered it necessary sometimes to have cast a temporary veil over the Statue of Liberty, she may again safely be shewn in an unimpaired lustre.

Of the following Verses I have nothing to say: if it should be decided that the greatness of the object cannot bear out the mediocrity of the execution, I will not appeal from the decision.

ODE

TO MY COUNTRY.

MDCCXCVIII.

S. 1.

Britons! hands and hearts prepare;
　The angry tempest threatens nigh,
Deep-ton'd thunders roll in air,
　Lightnings thwart the livid sky;
Thron'd upon the winged storm,
Fell Desolation rears her ghastly form,
Waves her black signal to her Hell-born brood,
And lures them thus with promised blood:

A. 1.

　" Drive, my Sons, the storm amain!
　　" Lo, the hated envied Land,
　" Where Piety and Order reign,
　　" And Freedom dares maintain her stand.
" Have ye not sworn, by night and hell,
" These from the earth for ever to expel?
" Rush on, resistless, to your destin'd prey,
" Death and Rapine point the way."

E. 1.

Britons! stand firm! with stout and dauntless heart
　Meet unappall'd the threatening boaster's rage;

Yours is the great, the unconquerable part
    For your lov'd hearths and altars to engage,
And sacred LIBERTY, more dear than life—
Yours be the triumph in the glorious strife.
Shall Theft and Murder braver deeds excite
Than honest scorn of shame and heavenly love of right?

S. 2.

Turn the bright historic page!
    Still in Glory's tented field
Albion's arms for many an age
    Have taught proud Gallia's Bands to yield.
Are not WE the Sons of those
Whose steel-clad Sires pursu'd the insulting foes
E'en to the centre of their wide domain,
And bow'd them to a Briton's reign?*

A. 2.

Kings in modest triumph led,
    Graced the SABLE VICTOR's arms:†
His conquering lance, the battle's dread;—
    His courtesy the conquer'd charms.
The lion-heart soft pity knows,
To raise with soothing cares his prostrate foes;
The vanquish'd head true Valour ne'er opprest,
Nor shunn'd to succour the distrest.

* Henry VI. crowned at Paris.
† The Black Prince.

E. 2.

Spirit of great Elizabeth ! inspire
   High thoughts, high deeds, worthy our ancient
      fame ;
Breathe through our ardent ranks the patriot fire,
   Kindled at Freedom's ever hallow'd flame;
Baffled and scorn'd, the Iberian Tyrant found,
Though half a world his iron sceptre bound,
The gallant Amazon could sweep away,
Arm'd with her people's love, the "Invincible" array.*

S. 3.

The Bold Usurper † firmly held
   The sword, by splendid treasons gain'd ;
And Gallia's fiery genius quell'd,
   And Spain's presumptuous claims restrain'd :
When lust of sway by flattery fed,‡
To venturous deeds the youthful Monarch led,
In the full flow of Victory's swelling tide
Britain check'd his power and pride.

A. 3.

To the great Batavian's name §
   Ceaseless hymns of triumph raise !
Scourge of tyrants, let his fame
   Live in songs of grateful praise.

* The Spanish Armada.   † Oliver Cromwell.
‡ Louis XIV.   § William III.

Thy turrets, Blenheim,* glittering to the sun,
Tell of bright fields from warlike Gallia won;
Tell how the mighty Monarch mourn'd in vain
His impious wish the world to chain.

E. 3.

And ye fam'd Heroes, late retir'd to heaven,
    Whose setting glories still the skies illume,
Bend from the blissful seats to virtue given —
    Avert your long-defended Country's doom.
Earth from her utmost bounds shall wondering tell
How Victory's meed ye gain'd, or conquering fell;
Britain's dread thunders bore from pole to pole,
Wherever man is found, or refluent oceans roll.

S. 4.

Names embalm'd in Honour's shrine,
    Sacred to immortal praise,
Patterns of Glory, born to shine
    In breathing arts or pictur'd lays:
See Wolfe by yielding numbers prest,
Expiring smile, and sink on Victory's breast!
See Minden's plains and Biscay's billowy bay
Deeds of deathless fame display.

A. 4.

O! tread with awe the sacred gloom,
    Patriot Virtue's last retreat;

* Blenheim, Ramilies, &c. &c.

Where Glory on the trophied tomb
  Joys their merit to repeat;
There Chatham lies, whose master-hand
Guided through seven bright years the mighty Band,
That round his urn, where grateful Memory weeps,
Each in his hallow'd marble sleeps.

E. 4.

Her brand accurs'd when Civil Discord hurl'd, *
  Britain alone the united world withstood,
Rodney his fortune-favour'd sails unfurl'd,
  And led three Nations' Chiefs to Thames's flood.
Firm on his Rock the Veteran Hero † stands;
  Beneath his feet unheeded thunders roar;
Smiling in scorn he sees the glittering Bands
  Fly with repulse and shame old Calpe's hopeless
    shore.

S. 5.

Heirs or partners of their toils,
  Matchless Heroes still we own;
Crown'd with honourable spoils
  From the leagued nations won.
On their high prows they proudly stand
The godlike Guardians of their native land;
Lords of the mighty deep triumphant ride,
Wealth and Victory at their side.

  * American War.   † Lord Heathfield.

A. 5.

Loyal, bold, and generous Bands,
    Strenuous in their Country's Cause,
Guard their cultivated Lands,
    Their Altars, Liberties, and Laws.
On his firm deep-founded throne
Great Brunswick sits, a name to fear unknown,
With brow erect commands the glorious strife,
Unaw'd, and prodigal of life.

E. 5.

Sons of fair Freedom's long-descended line,
    To Gallia's yoke shall Britons bend the neck—
No; in her Cause though Fate and Hell combine
    To bury all in universal wreck,
Of this fair Isle to make one dreary waste,
Her greatness in her ruins only traced,—
Arts, Commerce, Arms, sunk in one common grave—
The Man who dares to die, will never live a Slave.

No. XXIX.

May 28.

*In a former Number, we were enabled, by the communication
of a classical Correspondent, to compliment Citizen Muskein with an Address to his Gun-boats, imitated from a
favourite Ode of Horace.—Another (or perhaps the same)
hand, has obligingly furnished us with a Composition,
which we have no doubt will be equally acceptable to the
Citizen to whom it is addressed.*

ODE TO THE DIRECTOR MERLIN.

HORACE, B. I. O. 5.

Who now from Naples, Rome, or Berlin,
Creeps to thy blood-stain'd den, O Merlin,
    With diplomatic gold? to whom
    Dost thou give audience *en costume?*

AD PYRRHAM.

    Quis multâ gracilis te puer in rosâ
    Perfusus liquidis urget odoribus
      Grato, Pyrrha, sub antro?
      Cui flavam religas comam,

King-Citizen!—How sure each state,
That bribes thy love, shall feel thy hate;
   Shall see the Democratic storm
   Her Commerce, Laws, and Arts deform.

How credulous, to hope the bribe
Could purchase peace from Merlin's tribe!
   Whom faithless as the waves or wind,
   No oaths restrain, no treaties bind.

For us—beneath yon SACRED ROOF,
The NAVAL FLAGS and Arms of Proof
   By British Valour nobly bought,
   Shew how true safety must be sought!

Simplex Munditiis? Heu quoties fidem
Mutatosque Deos flebit, et aspera
   Nigris æquora ventis
   Emirabitur insolens,

Qui nunc te fruitur credulus aureâ:
Qui semper vacuam semper amabilem
   Sperat: nescius auræ
   Fallacis. Miseri, quibus

Intentata nites. Me tabulâ sacer
Votivâ paries indicat, uvida
   Suspendisse potenti
   Vestimenta maris Deo.

No. XXX.

June 4.

OUR ingenious Correspondent, Mr. HIGGINS, has not been idle. The deserved popularity of the Extracts, which we have been enabled to give from his two Didactic Poems, the PROGRESS OF MAN, and the LOVES OF THE TRIANGLES, has obtained for us the communication of several other works, which he has in hand, all framed upon the same principle, and directed to the same end. The propagation of the New System of Philosophy forms, as he has himself candidly avowed to us, the main object of all his writings. A system comprehending not Politics only, and Religion, but Morals and Manners, and generally whatever goes to the composition or holding together of Human Society; in all of which a total change and revolution is absolutely necessary (as he contends) for the advancement of our common nature to its true dignity, and to the summit of that perfection which the combination of matter, called MAN, is by its innate energies capable of attaining.

Of this System, while the sublimer and more scientific branches are to be taught by the splendid and striking medium of Didactic Poetry, or *ratiocination in rhyme*, illustrated with such paintings and portraitures

M

of Essences and their Attributes, as may lay hold of the
imagination, while they perplex the judgment;—the
more ordinary parts, such as relate to the conduct of
common life, and the regulation of social feelings, are
naturally the subject of a less elevated style of writing;—of a style which speaks to the eye as well as to
the ear,—in short, of Dramatic Poetry and Scenic Re-
presentation.

" With this view," says Mr. HIGGINS (for we love
to quote the very words of this extraordinary and in-
defatigable writer), "with this view" says he in a letter
dated from his study in St. Mary Axe, the window of
which looks upon the parish pump—" with this view, I
" have turned my thoughts more particularly to the
" German Stage; and have composed, in imitation of
" the most popular pieces of that country, which have
" already met with so general reception and admiration
" in this,—a Play: which, if It has a proper run, will,
" I think, do much to unhinge the present notions of
" men with regard to the obligations of Civil Society;
" and to substitute in lieu of a sober contentment, and
" regular discharge of the duties incident to each man's
" particular situation, a wild desire of undefinable lati-
" tude and extravagance,—an aspiration after shapeless
" somethings, that can neither be described nor un-
" derstood,—a contemptuous disgust at all that *is*, and
" a persuasion that nothing is as it ought to be;—to
" operate, in short, a general discharge of every man
" (in his own estimation) from every tie which laws
" divine or human, which local customs, immemorial

" habits, and multiplied examples impose upon him ;
" and to set them about doing what they like, where
" they like, when they like, and how they like,—with-
" out reference to any law but their own will, or to
" any consideration of how others may be affected by
" their conduct.

" When this is done, my dear Sir," continues Mr.
H. (for he writes very confidentially)—" You see that
" a great step is gained towards the dissolution of the
" frame of every existing community. I say nothing
" of *Governments*, as *their* fall is of course implicated in
" that of the Social System : — and you have long
" known, that I hold every Government (that acts by
" coercion and restriction—by laws made by the few
" to bind the many) as a *malum in se*,—an evil to be
" eradicated,—a nuisance to be abated,—by force, if
" force be practicable, if not,—by the artillery of rea-
" son--by pamphlets, speeches, toasts at Club-dinners,
" and though last, not least, by Didactic Poems.

" But where would be the advantage of the destruc-
" tion of this or that Government, if the form of So-
" ciety itself were to be suffered to continue such, as
" that another must necessarily arise out of it, and
" over it ?—Society, my dear Sir, in its present state,
" is a *hydra*. Cut off one head,—another presently
" sprouts out, and your labour is to begin again. At
" best, you can only hope to find it a *polypus*;—where,
" by cutting off the *head*, you are sometimes fortunate
" enough to find a *tail* (which answers all the same
" purposes) spring up in its place. This, we know,

" has been the case in France;—the only country in
" which the great experiment of regeneration has been
" tried with any thing like a fair chance of success.

" Destroy the frame of society,—decompose its parts,
" —and set the elements fighting one against another,
" —insulated and individual,—every man for himself
" (stripped of prejudice, of bigotry, and of feeling for
" others) against the remainder of his species;—and
" there is then some hope of a totally new *order of*
" *things*,—of a *Radical Reform* in the present corrupt
" System of the World.

" The German Theatre appears to proceed on this
" judicious plan. And I have endeavoured to con-
" tribute my mite towards extending its effect and its
" popularity. There is one obvious advantage attend-
" ing this mode of teaching;—that it can proportion
" the infractions of law, religion, or morality, which
" it recommends, to the capacity of a reader or spec-
" tator. If you tell a student, or an apprentice, or a
" merchant's clerk, of the virtue of a Brutus, or of
" the splendour of a La Fayette, you may excite his
" *desire* to be equally conspicuous; but how is he to
" set about it ? Where is he to find the tyrant to mur-
" der ? How is he to provide the monarch to be im-
" prisoned, and the national guards to be reviewed on
" a white horse ?—But paint the beauties of *forgery* to
" him in glowing colours;—shew him that the pre-
" sumption of virtue is in favour of rapine, and occa-
" sional murder on the highway;—and he presently
" understands you. The highway is at hand—the till

" or the counter is within reach. These *haberdash-*
" *ers' heroics* come home to the business and the bosoms
" of men. And you may readily make ten *footpads,*
" where you would not have materials nor opportunity
" for a single *tyrannicide.*

" The subject of the piece, which I herewith trans-
" mit to you, is taken from common or middling life ;
" and its merit, is that of teaching the most lofty truths
" in the most humble style, and deducing them from
" the most ordinary occurrences. Its moral is obvious
" and easy; and is one frequently inculcated by the
" German Dramas which I have had the good fortune
" to see ; being no other than " *the reciprocal duties of*
" *one or more husbands to one or more wives, and to the chil-*
" *dren who may happen to arise out of this complicated and*
" *endearing connection.*" The plot, indeed, is formed
" by the combination of the plots of *two* of the most
" popular of these plays (in the same way as Terence
" was wont to combine two stories of Menander's).
" The characters are such as the admirers of these
" plays will recognize for their familiar acquaintances.
" There are the usual ingredients of imprisonments,
" post-houses and horns, and appeals to angels and
" devils. I have omitted only the *swearing,* to which
" English ears are not yet sufficiently accustomed.

" I transmit at the same time a *Prologue,* which in
" some degree breaks the matter to the audience.
" About the song of Rogero, at the end of the first
" Act, I am less anxious than about any other part of
" the performance, as it is, in fact, literally translated

" from the composition of a young German friend of
" mine, an *Illuminé*, of whom I bought the original for
" three and sixpence. It will be a satisfaction to those
" of your Readers, who may not at first sight hit upon
" the tune, to learn, that it is setting by a hand of the
" first eminence.—I send also a rough sketch of the
" plot, and a few occasional notes.—The *Geography* is
" by the young Gentleman of the *Morning Chronicle*."

THE ROVERS;

OR,

THE DOUBLE ARRANGEMENT.

DRAMATIS PERSONÆ.

PRIOR *of the* ABBEY *of* QUEDLINBURGH, *very corpulent and cruel.*

ROGERO, *a Prisoner in the Abbey, in love with* MATILDA POTTINGEN.

CASIMERE, *a Polish Emigrant, in Dembrowsky's Legion, married to* CECILIA, *but having several Children by* MATILDA.

PUDDINGFIELD *and* BEEFFINGTON, *English Noblemen, exiled by the Tyranny of King John, previous to the signature of Magna Charta.*

RODERIC, *Count of* SAXE WEIMAR, *a bloody Tyrant, with red hair, and an amorous complexion.*

GASPAR, *the Minister of the Count*; *Author of* ROGERO'S *Confinement*.

Young POTTINGEN, *Brother to* MATILDA.

MATILDA POTTINGEN, *in love with* ROGERO, *and Mother to* CASIMERE'S *Children*.

CECILIA MÜCKENFELD, *Wife to* CASIMERE.

Landlady, Waiter, Grenadiers, Troubadours, &c. &c.

PANTALOWSKY, *and* BRITCHINDA, *Children of* MA-TILDA, *by* CASIMERE.

JOACHIM, JABEL, *and* AMARANTHA, *Children of* MA-TILDA, *by* ROGERO.

Children of CASIMERE *and* CECILIA, *with their respective Nurses*.

Several Children; *Fathers and Mothers unknown*.

The Scene lies in the Town of WEIMAR, *and the Neighbourhood of the* ABBEY *of* QUEDLINBURGH.

Time, from the 12th *to the present Century.*

PROLOGUE—*in Character.*

Too long the triumphs of our early times,
With civil discord and with regal crimes,
Have stain'd these boards; while Shakspeare's pen has
    shewn
Thoughts, manners, men, to modern days unknown.
Too long have Rome and Athens been *the rage*;
                     [*Applause.*
And classic Buskins soil'd a British Stage.

To-night our Bard, who scorns pedantic rules,
His Plot has borrow'd from the German schools;
—The German schools—where no dull maxims bind
The bold expansion of the electric mind.
Fix'd to no period, circled by no space,
He leaps the flaming bounds of time and place :
Round the dark confines of the forest raves,
With *gentle* Robbers * stocks his gloomy caves ;
Tells how Prime Ministers † are shocking things,
And *reigning Dukes* as bad as tyrant Kings ;
How to *two* swains ‡ *one* nymph her vows may give,
And how *two* damsels ‡ with *one* lover live !
Delicious scenes !—such scenes *our* Bard displays,
Which, crown'd with German, sue for British, praise.

* See the " Robbers," a German tragedy, in which Robbery is put in so fascinating a light, that the whole of a German University went upon the highway in consequence of it.

† See " Cabal and Love," a German tragedy, very severe against Prime Ministers, and reigning Dukes of Brunswick. —This admirable performance very judiciously reprobates the hire of German troops for the *American* War in the reign of Queen Elizabeth—a practice which would undoubtedly have been highly discreditable to that wise and patriotic Princess, not to say wholly unnecessary, there being no American War at that particular time.

‡ See the " Stranger; or, Reform'd Housekeeper," in which the former of these morals is beautifully illustrated; —and " Stella," a genteel German comedy, which ends with placing a man *bodkin* between *two wives*, like *Thames* between his *two banks*, in the Critic. Nothing can be more edifying than these two Dramas. I am shocked to hear that there are some people who think them ridiculous.

Slow are the steeds, that through Germania's roads
With hempen rein the slumbering post-boy goads;
Slow is the slumbering post-boy, who proceeds
Thro' deep sands floundering, on those tardy steeds;
More slow, more tedious, from his husky throat
Twangs through the twisted horn the struggling note.

These truths confess'd—Oh! yet, ye travell'd few,
Germania's *Plays* with eyes unjaundic'd view!
View and approve!—though in each passage fine
The faint translation * mock the genuine line,
Though the nice ear the erring sight belie,
For *U twice dotted* is pronounc'd like *I*;*   [*Applause.*
Yet oft the scene shall Nature's fire impart,
Warm *from* the breast, and glowing *to* the heart!

Ye travell'd few, attend!—On *you* our Bard
Builds his fond hope! Do you his genius guard!
                                                [*Applause.*

* These are the warnings very properly given to Readers,
to beware how they judge of what they cannot understand.
Thus, if the translation runs " *lightning of my soul, fulgura-*
" *tion of angels, sulphur of hell;*" we should recollect that
this is not coarse or strange in the German language, when
applied by a lover to his mistress; but the English has nothing precisely parallel to the original Mulychause Archan-
gelichen, which means rather *emanation of the archangelican
nature*—or to Smellmynkern Vankelfer, which if literally
rendered, would signify *made of stuff of the same odour whereof
the Devil makes flambeaux.* See Schüttenbrüch on the German Idiom.

Nor let succeeding generations say
—A British Audience *damn'd* a German Play!

> [*Loud and continued Applauses.*

Flash of Lightning.—The Ghost of PROLOGUE'S GRAND-
MOTHER *by the Father's side, appears to soft music, in a
white tiffany riding-hood.* PROLOGUE *kneels to receive
her blessing, which she gives in a solemn and affecting
manner, the Audience clapping and crying all the while.
—Flash of Lightning.—* PROLOGUE *and his* GRAND-
MOTHER *sink through the trap-door.*

THE ROVERS;

OR,

THE DOUBLE ARRANGEMENT.

ACT I.   SCENE I.

*Scene represents a Room at an Inn, at Weimar—On one side
of the Stage the Bar-room, with Jellies, Lemons in Nets,
Syllabubs, and part of a cold roast Fowl, &c.—On the
opposite side a Window looking into the Street, through
which Persons (Inhabitants of Weimar) are seen passing
to and fro in apparent agitation—Matilda appears in a
Great Coat and Riding Habit, seated at the corner of the
Dinner Table, which is covered with a clean Huckaback
Cloth—Plates and Napkins, with Buck's-Horn-handled
Knives and Forks, are laid as if for four Persons.*

Mat. Is it impossible for me to have dinner sooner?
Land. Madam, the Brunswick post-waggon is not yet
come in, and the Ordinary is never before two o'clock.

Mat. [*With a look expressive of disappointment, but immediately recomposing herself.*] Well, then, I must have patience. [*Exit Landlady.*] Oh Casimere!—How often have the thoughts of thee served to amuse these moments of expectation!—What a difference, alas!—Dinner—it is taken away as soon as over, and we regret it not!—It returns again with the return of appetite. —The beef of to-morrow will succeed to the mutton of to-day, as the mutton of to-day succeeded to the veal of yesterday.—But when once the heart has been occupied by a beloved object, in vain would we attempt to supply the chasm by another. How easily are our desires transferred from dish to dish!—Love only, dear, delusive, delightful Love, restrains our wandering appetites, and confines them to a particular gratification! . . . . . .

Post-horn blows, Re-enter Landlady.

Land. Madam, the post-waggon is just come in with only a single gentlewoman.

Mat. Then shew her up—and let us have dinner instantly; [*Landlady going*] and remember—[*after a moment's recollection, and with great earnestness*]—remember the toasted cheese. [*Exit Landlady,*

Cecilia enters, in a brown Cloth Riding-dress, as if just alighted from the Post-waggon.

Mat. Madam, you seem to have had an unpleasant journey, if I may judge from the dust on your riding-habit.

Cec. The way was dusty, Madam, but the weather was delightful. It recall'd to me those blissful moments when the rays of desire first vibrated through my soul.

Mat. [*Aside*] Thank heaven! I have at last found a heart which is in unison with my own [*to Cecilia*] —Yes, I understand you—the first pulsation of sentiment—the silver tones upon the yet unsounded harp. . . . . .

Cec. The dawn of life—when this blossom [*putting her hand upon her heart*] first expanded its petals to the penetrating dart of Love!

Mat. Yes—the time—the golden time, when the first beams of the morning meet and embrace one another!—The blooming blue upon the yet unplucked plum!— . . . . .

Cec. Your countenance grows animated, my dear Madam.

Mat. And yours too is glowing with illumination.

Cec. I had long been looking out for a congenial spirit!—my heart was withered—but the beams of yours have re-kindled it.

Mat. A sudden thought strikes me—Let us swear an eternal friendship.

Cec. Let us agree to live together!

Mat. Willingly.   [*with rapidity and earnestness.*

Cec. Let us embrace.   [*they embrace.*

Mat. Yes; I too have lov'd!—you, too, like me, have been forsaken!

          [*doubtingly, and as if with a desire to be informed.*

Cec. Too true!

Both. Ah these men! these men!

*Landlady enters, and places a Leg of Mutton on the Table,
with sour Krout and Pruin Sauce—then a small Dish of
Black Puddings.—Cecilia and Matilda appear to take no
notice of her.*

Mat. Oh Casimere!

Cec. [*Aside*] Casimere! that name!—Oh my heart,
how it is distracted with anxiety.

Mat. Heavens! Madam, you turn pale.

Cec. Nothing—a slight megrim—with your leave, I
will retire——

Mat. I will attend you.

   [*Exeunt Matilda and Cecilia. Manent Landlady and
      Waiter, with the Dinner on the Table.*

Land. Have you carried the dinner to the prisoner
in the vaults of the abbey?

Waiter. Yes.—Pease soup, as usual—with the scrag
end of a neck of mutton—the emissary of the Count
was here again this morning, and offered me a large
sum of money if I would consent to poison him.

Land. Which you refused? [*with hesitation and anxiety.*

Waiter. Can you doubt it?   [*with indignation.*

Land. [*recovering herself, and drawing up with an expression of dignity*] The conscience of a poor man is as
valuable to him as that of a prince. . . .

Waiter. It ought to be still more so, in proportion
as it is generally more pure.

Land. Thou say'st truly, Job.   . . . . .

Waiter. [*with enthusiasm*] He who can spurn at wealth when proffer'd as the price of crime, is greater than a prince.

Post-horn blows.   Enter Casimere (in a travelling dress— a light blue great coat with large metal buttons—his hair in a long queue, but twisted at the end; a large Keven- huller hat; a cane in his hand).

Cas. Here, Waiter, pull off my boots, and bring me a pair of slippers. [*Exit Waiter*] And heark'ye, my lad, a bason of water [*rubbing his hands*] and a bit of soap—I have not washed since I began my journey.

Waiter. [*answering from behind the door*] Yes, Sir.

Cas. Well, Landlady, what company are we to have?

Land. Only two gentlewomen, Sir.—They are just stept into the next room—they will be back again in a minute.

Cas. Where do they come from?

[*All this while the Waiter re-enters with the bason and water, Casimere pulls off his boots, takes a napkin from the table, and washes his face and hands.*

Land. There is one of them I think comes from Nu-remburgh.

Cas. [*Aside*] From Nuremburgh [*with eagerness*] her name?

Land. Matilda.

Cas. [*Aside*] How does this idiot woman torment me!—What else!

Land. I can't recollect.

Cas. Oh agony!   [*in a paroxysm of agitation.*

Waiter. See here, her name upon the travelling trunk
—Matilda Pottingen.

Cas. Ecstacy! ecstacy!   [*embracing the Waiter.*

Land. You seem to be acquainted with the lady—
shall I call her?

Cas. Instantly—instantly—tell her lov'd, her long
lost—tell her—

Land. Shall I tell her dinner is ready?

Cas. Do so—and in the mean while I will look after
my portmanteau.   [*Exeunt severally.*

*Scene changes to a subterraneous Vault in the Abbey of Qued-
linburgh;—with Coffins, 'Scutcheons, Death's Heads and
Cross-bones.—Toads, and other loathsome Reptiles are
seen traversing the obscurer parts of the Stage.—Rogero
appears, in chains, in a Suit of rusty Armour, with his
beard grown, and a Cap of a grotesque form upon his
head.—Beside him a Crock, or Pitcher, supposed to contain his daily allowance of sustenance.—A long silence,
during which the wind is heard to whistle through the
Caverns.—Rogero rises, and comes slowly forward, with
his arms folded.*

Rog. Eleven years! it is now eleven years since I
was first immured in this living sepulchre—the cruelty
of a Minister—the perfidy of a Monk—yes, Matilda!
for thy sake—alive amidst the dead—chained—coffined
—confined—cut off from the converse of my fellow-
men.—Soft!—what have we here? [*stumbles over a
bundle of sticks*] This cavern is so dark, that I can

scarcely distinguish the objects under my feet. Oh!
—the register of my captivity—Let me see, how stands
the account? [*Takes up the sticks, and turns them over
with a melancholy air; then stands silent for a few moments,
as if absorbed in calculation*] eleven years and fifteen days!
—Hah! the twenty-eighth of August! How does the
recollection of it vibrate on my heart! It was on this
day that I took my last leave of my Matilda. It was
a summer evening—her melting hand seemed to dis-
solve in mine, as I prest it to my bosom—Some demon
whispered me that I should never see her more.—I
stood gazing on the hated vehicle which was conveying her away for ever.—The tears were petrified under
my eyelids.—My heart was crystallized with agony —
Anon—I looked along the road.—The Diligence seemed to diminish every instant.—I felt my heart beat
against its prison, as if anxious to leap out and over-
take it.—My soul whirled round as I watched the rota-
tion of the hinder wheels.—A long trail of glory followed after her, and mingled with the dust—it was the
emanation of Divinity, luminous with love and beauty
—like the splendour of the setting sun—but it told me
that the sun of my joys was sunk for ever—Yes, here
in the depths of an eternal dungeon—in the nursing
cradle of hell—the suburbs of perdition—in a nest of
demons, where despair in vain sits brooding over the
putrid eggs of hope; where agony wooes the embrace
of death; where patience, beside the bottomless pool
of despondency, sits angling for impossibilities—Yet
even *here*, to behold her, to embrace her—Yes, Ma-

tilda, whether in this dark abode, amidst toads and spiders, or in a royal palace, amidst the more loathsome
reptiles of a Court, would be indifferent to me—Angels would shower down their hymns of gratulation
upon our heads—while fiends would envy the eter-
nity of suffering love . . . . Soft, what air was
that? it seemed a sound of more than human warb-
lings—Again [*listens attentively for some minutes*]—Only
the wind—It is well, however—it reminds me of that
melancholy air, which has so often solaced the hours
of my captivity—Let me see whether the damps of this
dungeon have not yet injured my guitar. [*Takes his
Guitar, tunes it, and begins the following Air with a full
accompaniment of Violins from the Orchestra.*

[*Air, Lanterna Magica.*]

SONG

BY ROGERO.

I.

Whene'er with haggard eyes I view
   This dungeon that I'm rotting in,
I think of those companions true
   Who studied with me at the U—
          —niversity of Gottingen,—
          —niversity of Gottingen.
   [*Weeps, and pulls out a blue kerchief, with which he
     wipes his eyes; gazing tenderly at it, he pro-
     ceeds—*

N

II.

Sweet kerchief, check'd with heav'nly blue,
    Which once my love sat knotting in!—
Alas! Matilda *then* was true!—
    At least I thought so at the U—
        —niversity of Gottingen—
        —niversity of Gottingen.
     [*At the repetition of this Line Rogero clanks his
     Chains in cadence.*

III.

Barbs! barbs! alas! how swift you flew
    Her neat post-waggon trotting in!
Ye bore Matilda from my view;
    Forlorn I languish'd at the U—
        —niversity of Gottingen—
        —niversity of Gottingen.

IV.

This faded form! this pallid hue!
    This blood my veins is clotting in,
My years are many—they were few
    When first I enter'd at the U—
        —niversity of Gottingen—
        —niversity of Gottingen.

V.

There first for thee my passion grew,
    Sweet! sweet Matilda Pottingen!

Thou wast the daughter of my Tu—
—tor, Law Professor at the U—
    —niversity of Gottingen—
    —niversity of Gottingen.

VI.

Sun, moon, and thou vain world, adieu,
    That kings and priests are plotting in :
Here doom'd to starve on water-gru—
—el * never shall I see the U —
    —niversity of Gottingen—
    —niversity of Gottingen.—

[*During the last Stanza Rogero dashes his head repeatedly
against the walls of his Prison; and, finally, so hard as
to produce a visible contusion. He then throws himself on
the floor in an agony. The Curtain drops—the Music
still continuing to play, till it is wholly fallen.*

* A manifest error—since it appears from the Waiter's
conversation (p. 173.), that Rogero was not doomed to starve
on water-gruel, but on pease-soup; which is a much better
thing. Possibly the length of Rogero's imprisonment had
impaired his memory; or he might wish to make things appear worse than they really were; which is very natural, I
think, in such a case as this poor unfortunate gentleman's.
                                    Printer's Devil.

No. XXXI.

June 11.

WE have received, in the course of the last week, several long, and to say the truth, dull letters, from unknown hands, reflecting, in very severe terms, on Mr. HIGGINS, for having, as it is affirmed, attempted to pass upon the world, as a faithful sample of the productions of the German Theatre, a performance no way resembling any of those pieces, which have of late excited, and which bid fair to engross the admiration of the British Public.

As we cannot but consider ourselves as the guardians of Mr. HIGGINS's literary reputation, in respect to every work of his which is conveyed to the world through the medium of our paper (though, what we think of the danger of his principles, we have already sufficiently explained for ourselves, and have, we trust, succeeded in putting our Readers upon their guard against them)—we hold ourselves bound not only to justify the fidelity of the imitation—but (contrary to our original intention) to give a further specimen of it in our present Number, in order to bring the question more fairly to issue between our Author and his calumniators.

In the first place, we are to observe, that Mr. HIG-
GINS professes to have taken his notion of German
plays wholly from the Translations which have appeared in our language.—If *they* are totally dissimilar from
the originals, Mr. H. may undoubtedly have been led
into error; but the fault is in the translators, not in
him. That he does not differ widely from the models
which he proposed to himself, we have it in our power
to prove satisfactorily; and might have done so in our
last Number, by subjoining to each particular passage
of his play, the scene in some one or other of the German plays, which he had in view when he wrote it.
These parallel passages were faithfully pointed out to
us by Mr. H. with that candour which marks his character; and if they were suppressed by us (as in truth
they were) on our heads be the blame, whatever it
may be. Little, indeed, did we think of the imputation which the omission would bring upon Mr. H. as
in fact, our principal reason for it, was the apprehension, that from the extreme closeness of the imitation
in most instances, he would lose in praise for invention, more than he would gain in credit for fidelity.

The meeting between Matilda and Cecilia, for example, in the First Act of the " Rovers," and their
sudden intimacy, has been censured as unnatural. Be
it so. It is taken *almost word for word*, from " Stella,"
a German (or professedly a German) piece now much
in vogue; from which also the catastrophe of Mr.
HIGGINS's play is in part borrowed, so far as relates
to the agreement to which the Ladies come, as the

Reader will see by and by, to share Casimere between them.

The dinner scene is copied partly from the published translation of the " Stranger," and partly from the first scene of " Stella." The song of Rogero, with which the first act concludes, is admitted on all hands to be in the very first taste ; and if no German original is to be found for it, so much the worse for the credit of German literature.

An objection has been made by one anonymous letter-writer, to the names of Puddingfield and Beefington, as little likely to have been assigned to English characters by any author of taste or discernment.   In answer to this objection, we have, in the first place, to admit that a small, and we hope not an unwarrantable, alteration has been made by us since the MS. has been in our hands.—These names stood originally Puddincrantz and Beefinstern, which sounded to our ears as being liable, especially the latter, to a ridiculous inflection—a difficulty that could only be removed by furnishing them with English terminations. With regard to the more substantial syllables of the names, our Author proceeded in all probability on the authority of Goldoni, who, though not a German, is an Italian writer of considerable reputation ; and who, having heard that the English were distinguished for their love of liberty and beef, has judiciously compounded the two words *Runnymede* and *beef*, and thereby produced an English nobleman, whom he styles *Lord Runnybeef*.

To dwell no longer on particular passages—the best way perhaps of explaining the whole scope and view of Mr. H.'s imitation, will be to transcribe the short sketch of the plot, which that Gentleman transmitted to us, together with his Drama, and which it is perhaps the more necessary to give at length, as the limits of our paper not allowing of the publication of the whole piece, some general knowledge of its main design may be acceptable to our Readers, in order to enable them to judge of the several Extracts which we lay before them.

PLOT.

Rogero, son of the late Minister of the Count of Saxe Weimar, having, while he was at college, fallen desperately in love with Matilda Pottingen, daughter of his tutor, Doctor Engelbertus Pottingen, Professor of Civil Law; and Matilda evidently returning his passion, the Doctor, to prevent ill consequences, sends his daughter on a visit to her Aunt in Wetteravia, where she becomes acquainted with Casimere, a Polish Officer, who happens to be quartered near her Aunt's; and has several children by him.

Roderic, Count of Saxe Weimar, a Prince of a tyrannical and licentious disposition, has for his Prime Minister and favourite, Gaspar, a crafty villain, who had risen to his post by first ruining, and then putting to death, Rogero's father. —Gaspar, apprehensive of the power and popularity which the young Rogero may enjoy at his return to Court, seizes the occasion of his intrigue with Matilda (of which he is apprized officially by Doctor Pottingen) to procure from his

Master an order for the recall of Rogero from college, and for committing him to the care of the Prior of the Abbey of Quedlinburgh, a Priest, rapacious, savage, and sensual, and devoted to Gaspar's interests —sending at the same time private orders to the Prior to confine him in a dungeon.

Here Rogero languishes many years. His daily sustenance is administered to him through a grated opening at the top of a cavern, by the Landlady of the Golden Eagle at Weimar, with whom Gaspar contracts, in the Prince's name, for his support; intending, and more than once endeavouring, to corrupt the Waiter to mingle poison with the food, in order that he may get rid of Rogero for ever.

In the mean time Casimere, having been called away from the neighbourhood of Matilda's residence to other quarters, becomes enamoured of, and marries Cecilia, by whom he has a family; and whom he likewise deserts after a few years co-habitation, on pretence of business which calls him to Kamtschatka.

Doctor Pottingen, now grown old and infirm, and feeling the want of his daughter's society, sends young Pottingen in search of her, with strict injunctions not to return without her; and to bring with her either her present lover Casimere, or, should that not be possible, Rogero himself, if he can find him; the Doctor having set his heart upon seeing his children comfortably settled before his death. Matilda, about the same period, quits her Aunt's in search of Casimere; and Cecilia having been advertised (by an anonymous letter) of the falsehood of his Kamschatka journey, sets out in the post-waggon on a similar pursuit.

It is at this point of time the Play opens—with the accidental meeting of Cecilia and Matilda at the Inn at Weimar. Casimere arrives there soon after, and falls in first with Matilda, and then with Cecilia. Successive *éclaircissements* take place, and an arrangement is finally made, by which the two Ladies are to live jointly with Casimere.

Young Pottingen, wearied with a few weeks search, during which he has not been able to find either of the objects of it, resolves to stop at Weimar, and wait events there. It so happens that he takes up his lodging in the same house with Puddincrantz and Beefinstern, two English Noblemen, whom the tyranny of King John has obliged to fly from their country; and who, after wandering about the Continent for some time, have fixed their residence at Weimar.

The news of the signature of Magna Charta arriving, determines Puddincrantz and Beefinstern to return to England. Young Pottingen opens his case to them, and intreats them to stay to assist him in the object of his search.—This they refuse; but coming to the Inn where they are to set off for Hamburgh, they meet Casimere, from whom they had both received many civilities in Poland.

Casimere, by this time, tired of his "DOUBLE ARRANGE-"MENT," and having learnt from the Waiter that Rogero is confined in the vaults of the neighbouring Abbey *for love*, resolves to attempt his rescue, and to make over Matilda to him as the price of his deliverance. He communicates his scheme to Puddingfield and Beefington, who agree to assist him; as also does Young Pottingen. The Waiter of the Inn proving to be a *Knight Templar* in disguise, is appointed leader of the expedition. A band of Troubadours, who happen to be returning from the Crusades, and a Company of Austrian and Prussian Grenadiers returning from the Seven Years' War, are engaged as troops.

The attack on the Abbey is made with success. The Count of Weimar and Gaspar, who are feasting with the

Prior, are seized and beheaded in the Refectory. The Prior
is thrown into the dungeon, from which Rogero is rescued.
Matilda and Cecilia rush in. The former recognizes Rogero, and agrees to live with him. The Children are produced on all sides—and Young Pottingen is commissioned
to write to his father, the Doctor, to detail the joyful events
which have taken place, and to invite him to Weimar to partake of the general felicity.

THE ROVERS;

OR,

THE DOUBLE ARRANGEMENT.

ACT II.

Scene—a Room in an ordinary Lodging-House, at WEIMAR.
*—*PUDDINGFIELD *and* BEEFINGTON *discovered, sitting at a small deal Table, and playing at All-Fours.
Young* POTTINGEN, *at another Table in the corner of
the Room, with a Pipe in his Mouth, and a Saxon Mug
of a singular shape beside him, which he repeatedly applies
to his lips, turning back his head, and casting his eyes
towards the Firmament—at the last trial he holds the
Mug for some moments in a directly inverted position; then
replaces it on the Table, with an air of dejection, and gradually sinks into a profound slumber.—The Pipe falls
from his hand, and is broken.—*

Beef. I beg.

Pudd. [*deals three Cards to Beefington*] Are you satisfied ?

Beef. Enough. What have you?

Pudd. High—Low—and the Game.

Beef. Damnation! 'tis my deal. [*deals—turns up a knave*] One for his heels! [*triumphantly.*

Pudd. Is king highest?

Beef. No. [*sternly*] The game is mine. The knave gives it me.

Pudd. Are knaves so prosperous?

Beef. Ay marry are they in this world. They have the game in their hands. Your kings are but *noddies* * to them.

Pudd. Ha! Ha! Ha!—Still the same proud spirit, Beefington, which procured thee thine exile from England.

Beef. England! my native land!—when shall I revisit thee?

[*during this time Puddingfield deals and begins to arrange his hand.*

Beef. [*continues*] Phoo—Hang All-Fours; what are they to a mind ill at ease?—Can they cure the heart-ache?—Can they sooth banishment?—Can they lighten

---

* This is an excellent joke in German; the point and spirit of which is but ill-*Rendered* in a translation. A NODDY, the Reader will observe, has two significations—the one a *knave at All-fours*: the other a *fool* or *booby*. See the translation by Mr. Render of Count Benyowsky, or the Conspiracy of Kamschatka, a German Tragi-Comi-Comi-Tragedy; where the play opens with a Scene of a Game at Chess (from which the whole of this Scene is copied) and a joke of the same point, and merriment about Pawns, *i. e.* Boors being *a match for* Kings.

ignominy?—Can All-Fours do this?—O! my Puddingfield, thy limber and lightsome spirit bounds up
against affliction—with the elasticity of a well bent
bow; but mine—O! mine—

> [*falls into an agony, and sinks back in his Chair.
> Young Pottingen, awakened by the noise, rises, and
> advances with a grave demeanour towards Beefing-
> ton and Puddingfield. The former begins to reco-
> ver.*

Y. Pot. What is the matter Comrades?*—you seem
agitated. Have you lost or won?

Beef. Lost.—I have lost my country.

Y. Pot. And I my sister.—I came hither in search
of her.

Beef. O, England!

Y. Pot. O, Matilda!

Beef. Exiled by the tyranny of an Usurper, I seek
the means of revenge, and of restoration to my country.

Y. Pot. Oppressed by the tyranny of an Abbot, per-
secuted by the jealousy of a Count, the betrothed husband of my sister languishes in a loathsome captivity
—Her lover is fled no one knows whither—and I, her
brother, am torn from my paternal roof and from my
studies in chirurgery; to seek him and her, I know

---

* This word in the original is strictly *fellow-lodgers*—
"*Co-occupants of the same room, in a house let out at a small rent
by the week.*"—There is no single word in English which
expresses so complicated a relation, except perhaps the cant
term of *chum*, formerly in use at our Universities.

not where—to rescue Rogero, I know not how. Comrades, your counsel—my search fruitless—my money gone—my baggage stolen! What am I to do?—In yonder Abbey—in these dark, dank vaults, there, my friends—there lies Rogero—there Matilda's heart—

SCENE II.

Enter Waiter.

Waiter. Sir, here is a person who desires to speak with you.

Beef. [*Goes to the door, and returns with a Letter, which he opens—On perusing it his countenance becomes illuminated, and expands prodigiously*] Hah, my friend, what joy!

[*turning to Puddingfield.*

Pudd. What? tell me—let your Puddingfield partake it.

Beef. See here—   [*produces a printed Paper.*
Pudd. What?—   [*with impatience.*
Beef. [*in a significant tone*] A newspaper!

Pudd. Hah, what sayst thou!—A newspaper!

Beef. Yes, Puddingfield, and see here [*shews it partially*] from England.

Pudd. [*with extreme earnestness*] Its name!

Beef. The *Daily Advertiser*—

Pudd. Oh ecstasy!

Beef. [*with a dignified severity*] Puddingfield, calm yourself—repress those transports—remember that you are a man.

Pudd. [*after a pause with suppressed emotion*] Well, I

will be—I am calm—yet tell me, Beefington, does it contain any news?

Beef. Glorious news, my dear Puddingfield—the Barons are victorious—King John has been defeated —Magna Charta, that venerable immemorial inheritance of Britons, was signed last Friday was three weeks, the third of July Old Style.

Pudd. I can scarce believe my ears—but let me satisfy my eyes—shew me the paragraph.

Beef. Here it is, just above the advertisements.

Pudd. [*reads*] " The great demand for Packwood's Razor Straps"—

Beef. 'Pshaw! what, ever blundering—you drive me from my patience—see here, at the head of the column.

Pudd. [*reads*]

" A hireling Print, devoted to the Court,
" Has dared to question our veracity
" Respecting the events of yesterday;
" But by to-day's accounts, our information
" Appears to have been perfectly correct.
" The Charter of our Liberties receiv'd
" The Royal Signature at five o'clock,
" When Messengers were instantly dispatch'd
" To Cardinal Pandulfo; and their Majesties,
" After partaking of a cold collation,
" Return'd to Windsor."—I am satisfied.

Beef. Yet here again—there are some further particulars [*turns to another part of the Paper*] " Extract of " a Letter from Egham—" My dear Friend, we are

" all here in high spirits—the interesting event which
" took place this morning at Runnymede, in the neigh-
" bourhood of this town"—

Pudd. Hah! Runnymede—enough—no more—my
doubts are vanished—then are we free indeed!—

Beef. I have, besides, a Letter in my pocket from
our Friend, the immortal Bacon, who has been appointed Chancellor.—Our outlawry is reversed!—what
says my Friend—shall we return by the next packet?

Pudd. Instantly, instantly!

Both. Liberty!—Adelaide!—revenge!

[*Exeunt—Young Pottingen following, and waving his
Hat, but obviously without much consciousness of the
meaning of what has passed.*

*Scene changes to the outside of the Abbey. A Summer's Even-
ing—Moonlight.*

*Companies of Austrian and Prussian Grenadiers march
across the stage, confusedly, as if returning from the
Seven Years' War. Shouts and martial Music.*

*The Abbey gates are opened. The Monks are seen passing
in procession, with the Prior at their head. The Choir is
heard chaunting Vespers. After which a pause. Then
a Bell is heard, as if ringing for supper. Soon after, a
noise of singing and jollity.*

*Enter from the Abbey, pushed out of the gates by the Porter,
a* TROUBADOUR, *with a bundle under his cloak, and a*
LADY *under his arm.* TROUBADOUR *seems much in
liquor, but caresses the* FEMALE MINSTREL.

Fem. Min. Trust me, Gieronymo, thou seemest melancholy. What hast thou got under thy cloak?

Trou. 'Pshaw, women will be inquiring. Melancholy! not I.—I will sing thee a song, and the subject of it shall be thy question—" what have I got under my cloak?" It is a riddle, Margaret—I learnt it of an Almanac-maker at Gotha—if thou guessest it after the first stanza, thou shalt have never a drop for thy pains. Hear me—and, d'ye mark! twirl thy thingumbob while I sing.

Fem. Min. 'Tis a pretty tune, and hums dolefully.

                 [*Plays on her Balalaika.**
                 Troubadour sings.

      I bear a secret comfort *here*,
         [*putting his hand on the bundle, but without
           shewing it.*
      A joy I'll ne'er impart;
      It is not wine, it is not beer,
        But it consoles my heart.

Fem. Min. [*interrupting him*] I'll be hang'd if you don't mean the bottle of cherry-brandy that you stole out of the vaults in the Abbey cellar.

Trou. I mean!—Peace, wench, thou disturbest the current of my feelings—

         [*Fem. Min. attempts to lay hold on the bottle. Trou-*

---

* The Balalaika is a Russian instrument, resembling the guitar.—See the Play of " Count Benyowsky," *Rendered* into English.

badour pushes her aside, and continues singing without interruption.]

This cherry-bounce, this lov'd noyau,
   My drink for ever be ;
But, sweet my love, thy wish forego ;
   I'll give no drop to thee !

          [*Both together,*]

Trou. { This } cherry-bounce { this } lov'd noyau,
F. M. { That }   { that }

Trou. { My } drink for ever be ;
F. M. { Thy }

Trou. } But, sweet my love, { thy wish forego !
F. M. }   { one drop bestow.

Trou. { I   } keep it all for { me !
F. M. { Nor }   { thee !

[*Exeunt struggling for the bottle, but without anger or animosity, the Fem. Min. appearing by degrees to obtain a superiority in the contest.*

END OF ACT II.

Act the Third—contains the eclaircissements and final arrangement between Casimere, Matilda, and Cecilia ; which so nearly resemble the concluding Act of " Stella," that we forbear to lay it before our Readers.

O

ACT IV.

*Scene—the Inn door—Diligence drawn up. Casimere ap-
pears superintending the package of his Portmanteaus,
and giving directions to the Porters.*

Enter Beefington and Puddingfield.

Pudd. Well, Coachey, have you got two inside
places?

Coach. Yes, your Honour.

Pudd. [*seems to be struck with Casimere's appearance.
He surveys him earnestly, without paying any attention to the
Coachman, then doubtingly pronounces*] Casimere!

Cas. [*turning round rapidly, recognizes Puddingfield,
and embraces him.*

Cas. My Puddingfield!

Pudd. My Casimere!

Cas. What, Beefington too! [*discovering him*] then is
my joy complete.

Beef. Our fellow-traveller, as it seems?

Cas. Yes, Beefington—but wherefore to Hamburgh?

Beef. Oh, Casimere *—to fly—to fly—to return—

* See "Count Benyowsky: or, the Conspiracy of Kamschatka," where Crustiew, an old gentleman of much saga-
city, talks the following nonsense.

Crustiew. [*with youthful energy and an air of secrecy and
confidence*] "To fly, to fly, to the isles of Marian—the island
" of Tinian—a terrestrial paradise. Free—free—a mild cli-
" mate—a new-created sun—wholesome fruits—harmless
" inhabitants—and Liberty—tranquillity."

England—our country—Magna Charta—it is liberated
—a new æra—House of Commons—Crown and Anchor—Opposition—

Cas. What a contrast! you are flying to Liberty and
your home—I driven from my home by tyranny—am
exposed to domestic slavery in a foreign country.

Beef. How domestic slavery?

Cas. Too true—two wives [*slowly, and with a dejected
air—then after a pause*]—you knew my Cecilia?

Pudd. Yes, five years ago.

Cas. Soon after that period I went upon a visit to a
Lady in Wetteravia—my Matilda was under her protection—alighting at a peasant's cabin, I saw her on a
charitable visit, spreading bread and butter for the
children, in a light blue riding habit. The simplicity
of her appearance—the fineness of the weather—all con-
spired to interest me—my heart moved to hers—as if
by a magnetic sympathy—we wept, embraced, and went
home together—she became the mother of my Pantalowsky. But five years of enjoyment have not stifled
the reproaches of my conscience—her Rogero is lan-
guishing in captivity—if I could restore her to *him!*

Beef. Let us rescue him.

Cas. Will without power,* is like children playing
at soldiers.

Beef. Courage without power,† is like a consump-
tive running footman.

* See "Count Benyowsky," as before.
† See "Count Benyowsky."

Cas. Courage without power is a contradiction.*—
Ten brave men might set all Quedlinburgh at defi-
ance.

Beef. Ten brave men—but where are they to be
found?

Cas. I will tell you—marked you the Waiter?

Beef. The Waiter?—   [*doubtingly.*

Cas. [*in a confidential tone*] No Waiter, but a *Knight
Templar.* Returning from the Crusade, he found his
Order dissolved, and his person proscribed. He dissembled his rank, and embraced the profession of a
Waiter. I have made sure of him already. There
are, besides, an Austrian and a Prussian Grenadier.
I have made them abjure their national enmity, and
they have sworn to fight henceforth in the cause of
Freedom. These, with Young Pottingen, the Waiter,
and ourselves, make seven—the Troubadour, with his
two attendant Minstrels, will complete the ten.

Beef. Now then for the execution. [*with enthusiasm.*

Pudd. Yes, my boys—for the execution.

                         [*clapping them on the back.*

Waiter. But hist! we are observed.

Trou. Let us by a song conceal our purposes.

---

* See "Count Benyowsky" again. From which Play this
and the preceding references are taken word for word. We
acquit the Germans of such reprobate silly stuff. It must be
the translator's.

RECITATIVE ACCOMPANIED.*

Cas. Hist! hist! nor let the airs that blow
    From Night's cold lungs, our purpose know!
Pudd. Let Silence, mother of the dumb,
Beef. Press on each lip her palsied thumb!
Wait. Let Privacy, allied to Sin,
    That loves to haunt the tranquil inn—
Gren. } And Conscience start, when she shall view,
Trou. } The mighty deed we mean to do!

GENERAL CHORUS—*Con spirito.*

Then Friendship swear, ye faithful Bands,
    Swear to save a shackled hero!
See where yon Abbey frowning stands!
    Rescue, rescue, brave Rogero!
Cas. Thrall'd in a Monkish tyrant's fetters
    Shall great Rogero hopeless lie?
Y. Pot. In my pocket I have letters,
    Saying, "help me, or I die!"

Allegro Allegretto.

Cas. Beef. Pudd. Gren. }
Trou. Waiter, and Pot. } Let us fly, let us fly,
with enthusiasm } Let us help, ere he die!

    [*Exeunt omnes, waving their hats.*

* We believe this song to be copied, with a small varia-
tion in metre and meaning, from a song in "Count Benyowsky; or, the Conspiracy of Kamschatka,"—where the conspirators join in a chorus, *for fear of being overheard.*

*Scene—the Abbey Gate, with Ditches, Drawbridges, and
Spikes. Time—about an hour before Sunrise. The Conspirators appear as if in ambuscade, whispering, and con-
sulting together, in expectation of the Signal for attack.
The WAITER is habited as a Knight Templar, in the dress
of his Order, with the Cross on his breast, and the Scal-
lop on his shoulder. PUDDINGFIELD and BEEFING-
TON armed with Blunderbusses and Pocket-pistols; the
GRENADIERS in their proper Uniforms. The TROU-
BADOUR with his attendant Minstrels, bring up the rear
—martial Music—the Conspirators come forward, and
present themselves before the Gate of the Abbey.—Alarum
—firing of Pistols—the Convent appear in Arms upon the
Walls—the Drawbridge is let down—a Body of Choristers
and Lay-brothers attempt a Sally, but are beaten back
and the Verger killed. The besieged attempt to raise
the Drawbridge—PUDDINGFIELD and BEEFINGTON
press forward with alacrity, throw themselves upon the
Drawbridge, and by the exertion of their weight, preserve
it in a state of depression—the other besiegers join them,
and attempt to force the entrance, but without effect. PUD-
DINGFIELD makes the signal for the battering ram. Enter QUINTUS CURTIUS and MARCUS CURIUS
DENTATUS, in their proper Military Habits, preceded
by the Roman Eagle—the rest of their Legion are employed
in bringing forward a battering ram, which plays for a
few minutes to slow time, till the entrance is forced. After
a short resistance, the besiegers rush in with shouts of Victory.*

*Scene changes to the interior of the Abbey.   The inhabitants
    of the Convent are seen flying in all directions.*

The COUNT *of* WEIMAR *and the* PRIOR, *who had been
    found feasting in the Refectory, are brought in manacled.
    The* COUNT *appears transported with rage, and gnaws
    his chains. The* PRIOR *remains insensible, as if stupified
    with grief.* BEEFINGTON *takes the keys of the Dun-
    geon, which are hanging at the* PRIOR'S *girdle, and
    makes a sign for them both to be led away into confinement
    —Exeunt* PRIOR *and* COUNT *properly guarded. The
    rest of the Conspirators disperse in search of the Dungeon
    where* ROGERO *is confined.*

END OF ACT THE FOURTH.

No. XXXII.

June 18.

We are indebted for the following Imitation of Catullus, to a literary Correspondent. Whether it will remove the doubts we formerly expressed, of Citizen Muskein's acquaintance with the Classics, from the minds of our Readers, we cannot pretend to say. It is given to us as a faithful translation from the French—as such, we present it to our Readers; premising only, that though the Citizen Imitator seems to have Sans-cullottized the original in two or three places, yet he every where expresses himself with a naiveté and truth, in his verse, that we seek for in vain, in many of his Countrymen, who have recorded their victories and defeats in very vulgar prose.

AN AFFECTIONATE EFFUSION OF CITIZEN MUS-KEIN, TO HAVRE-DE-GRACE.

Fairest of cities,* which the Seine
Surveys 'twixt Paris and the main,
Sweet Havre! sweetest Havre, hail!
How gladly with my tatter'd sail,†

AD SIRMIONEM PENINSULAM.

* Peninsularum Sirmio, Insularumque,
  Ocelle! quascunque in liquentibus stagnis,
  Marique vasto fert uterque Neptunus;
† Quam te libenter, quamque lætus inviso,

Yet trembling from this wild adventure,
Do I thy friendly harbour enter!

   Well—now I've leisure, let me see
What boats are left me; one, two, three—
Bravo! the better half remain;
And all my Heroes are not slain.
And if my senses don't deceive,
I too am safe,*—yes, I believe,
Without a wound I reach thy shore;
(For I have felt myself all o'er)
I've all my limbs, and, be it spoken
With honest triumph, no bone broken—

   How pleasing is the sweet transition †
From this vile Gun-boat Expedition;
From winds and waves, and wounds and scars,
From British Soldiers, British Tars,
To his own house, where, free from danger,
Muskein may live at rack and manger;
May stretch his limbs in his own cot,‡
Thankful he has not gone to pot;

   Vix mî ipse credens Thyniam, atque Bithynos
   Liquisse campos,* et videre te in tuto.

† O quid solutis est beatius curis,
   Quom mens onus reponit, ac peregrino
   Labore fessi venimus larem ad nostrum,
‡ Desideratoque acquiescimus lecto.

Nor for the bubble glory strive,
But bless himself that he's alive!

Havre,* sweet Havre! hail again,
O! bid thy sons (a frolic train,†
Who under Chenier welcom'd in
With dance and song, the *Guillotine*),
In long procession seek the strand;
For Muskein now prepares to land,
'Scap'd, Heav'n knows how, from that curs'd crew
That haunt the Rocks of SAINT MARCOU.

   * Salve! O venusta Sirmio! atque hero gaude!
     Gaudete! vosque Lydiæ lacus undæ!
     Ridete † quicquid est domi cachinnorum!

No. XXXIII.

June 25.

AFTER the splendid account of Buonaparte's successes in the East, which our Readers will find in another part of this Paper, and which they will peruse with equal wonder and apprehension, it is some consolation to us to have to state, not only from authority, but in verse, that our Government has not been behind hand with that of France ; but that, aware of the wise and enterprizing spirit of the Enemy, and of the danger which might arise to our distant possessions from the export of Learning and learned Men being entirely in their hands, Ministers have long ago determined on an expedition of a similar nature, and have actually embarked at Portsmouth, on board one of the East-India Company's ships, taken up for that purpose (the ship Capricorn, Mr. Thomas Truman, Commander), several tons of *Savans*, the growth of this country.   The whole was conducted with the utmost secrecy and dispatch, and it was not till we were favoured with the following copy of a Letter (obligingly communicated to us by the Tunisian gentleman to whom it is addressed) that we had any suspicion of the extent and nature of the design, or indeed of any such design being in contemplation.

The several great names which are combined to render this Expedition the most surprising and splendid ever undertaken, could not indeed have been spared from the country to which they are an ornament, for any other purpose, than one the most obviously connected with the interests of the empire, and the most widely beneficial to mankind.

The secrecy with which they have been withdrawn from the British Public, without being so much as missed or inquired after, reflects the highest honour on the planners of the Enterprize. Even the celebrity of Doctor P—r has not led to any discovery or investigation : the silent admirers of that great man have never once thought of asking what was become of him; —till it is now all at once come to light, that he has been for weeks past on ship-board, the brightest star in the bright constellation of talents which stud the quarter-deck of the Capricorn, Mr. T. Truman (as before mentioned) Commander.

The resignation of the late worthy President of a certain Agricultural Board, might indeed have taught mankind to look for some extraordinary event in the world of science and adventure ; and those who had the good fortune to see the deportation from his house, of the several wonderful anomalies which had for years formed its most distinguished inmates,—the stuffed ram, the dried boar, the cow with three horns, and other fanciful productions of a like nature, could not but speculate with some degree of seriousness on the purpose of their removal, and on the place of their destination.

It now appears, that there was in truth no light object in view. They were destined, with the rest of the *Savans*, on whom this Country prides itself (and long may it have reason to indulge the honest exultation) to undertake a voyage of no less grandeur than peril ; to counteract the designs of the Directory, and to frustrate or forestall the Conquests of Buonaparte.

The young Gentleman who writes the following Letter to his Friend in London, is, as may be seen, interpreter to the Expedition. We have understood further, that he is nearly connected with the young man who writes for the *Morning Chronicle*, and conducts the *Critical*, *Argumentative*, and *Geographical* Departments. —Some say it is the young man himself, who has assumed a feigned name, and, under the disguise of a Turkish dress and circumcision, is gone, at the express instigation of his employers, to improve himself in geographical knowledge. We have our doubts upon this subject, as we think we recognize the style of this deplorable young man, in an article of last week's *Morning Chronicle*, which we have had occasion to answer in a preceding column of our present Paper. Be that as it may, the information contained in the following Letter may be depended upon.

We cannot take leave of the subject, without remarking what a fine contrast and companion the Vessel and Cargo described in the following Poem, affords

to the " NAVIS STULTIFERA," the " SHIPPE OF
" FOOLES" of the celebrated Barclay; and we cannot forbear hoping, that the Argenis of an Author of
the same name may furnish a hint for an account of
this stupendous Expedition in a learned language, from
the only pen which in modern days is capable of writing Latin with a purity and elegance worthy of so ex-
alted a theme; and that the Author of a classical *Pre-*
face may become the Writer of a no less celebrated
Voyage.

TRANSLATION OF A LETTER
(IN ORIENTAL CHARACTERS)
FROM BAWBA-DARA-ADUL-PHOOLA,
DRAGOMAN TO THE EXPEDITION,
TO NEEK-AWL-ARETCHID-KOOEZ,
SECRETARY TO THE TUNISIAN EMBASSY.

DEAR NEEK-AWL,

You'll rejoice, that at length I am able
To date these few lines from the Captain's own table.
Mr. Truman himself, of his proper suggestion,
Has in favour of science decided the question;
So we walk the main-deck, and are mess'd with the
        Captain;
I leave you to judge of the joy we are rapt in.

At Spithead they embark'd us; how precious a cargo!
And we sail'd before day, to escape the embargo.
There was Sh—b—h, the wonderful mathematician;
And D—rw—n, the poet, the sage, and physician;
There was B—dd—s, and Bru—n, and G—dw—n whose
	trust is,
He may part with his work on *Political Justice*
To some Iman or Bonze, or Judaical Rabbin;
So with huge quarto volumes he piles up the cabin.
There was great Dr. P—r, whom we style Bellendenus;
The Doctor and I have a hammock between us.
'Tis a little unpleasant thus crowding together,
On account of the motion, and heat of the weather;
Two souls in one birth they oblige us to cram,
And Sir John *will* insist on a place for his ram.
Though the Doctor, I find, is determined to think
'Tis the animal's hide that occasions the stink;
In spite of the' experienced opinion of Truman,
Who contends that the scent is exclusively human.
But B—dd—s and D—rw—n engage to repair
This slight inconvenience with *oxygene air.*

Whither bound? (you will ask) 'tis a question, my
	friend,
On which I long doubted; my doubt's at an end.
To Arabia the Stony, Sabæa the Gummy,
To the land where each man that you meet is a mummy;
To the mouths of the Nile, to the banks of Araxes,
To the *Red,* and the *Yellow,* the *White,* and the *Black*
	seas,

With telescopes, globes, and a quadrant, and sextant,
And the works of all authors whose writings are extant;
With surveys and plans, topographical maps,
Theodolites, watches, spring-guns, and steel traps,
Phials, crucibles, air pumps, electric machinery,
And pencils for painting the natives and scenery.
In short, we are sent to oppose all we know,
To the knowledge and mischievous arts of the foe,
Who, though placing in arms a well-grounded reliance,
Go to war with a flying artill'ry of science.

The French *Savans*, it seems, recommended this
    measure,
With a view to replenish the national treasure.
First, the true *Rights of Man* they will preach in all
    places,
But chief (when 'tis found) in the Egyptian Oasis:
And this doctrine, 'tis hoped, in a very few weeks
Will persuade the wild Arabs to murder their Cheiks,
And, to aid the *Great Nation's* beneficent plans,
Plunder pyramids, catacombs, towns, caravans,
Then inlist under Arcole's gallant Commander,
Who will conquer the world like his model Iskander.
His army each day growing bolder and finer,
With the Turcoman tribes he subdues Asia Minor,
Beats Paul and his Scythians, his journey pursues
Cross the Indus, with tribes of Armenians, and Jews,
And Bucharians, and Affghans, and Persians, and
    Tartars,—
Chokes the wretched Mogul in his Grandmother's
    garters,

And will hang him to dry in the Luxemburg Hall,
'Midst the plunder of Carthage and spoils of Bengal.

   Such, we hear, was the plan : but I trust, if we meet
     'em,
That, *Savant* to *Savant*, our Cargo will beat 'em.
Our plan of proceeding, I'll presently tell :—
But soft—I am call'd—I must bid you farewell ;—
To attend on our *Savans* my pen I resign—
For, it seems, that they *duck* them on *crossing* the Line.

   We deeply regret this interruption of our Oriental
Poet, and the more so, as the Prose Letters which we
have received from a less learned Correspondent, do
not enable us to explain the tactics of our belligerent
philosophers so distinctly as we could have wished. It
appears in general, that the learned Doctor who has
the honour of sharing the hammock of the amiable Oriental, trusted principally to his superior knowledge in
the Greek language, by means of which he hoped to
entangle his antagonists in inextricable confusion. Dr.
D——n proposed (as might be expected) his celebrated
experiment of the ice-island, which, being towed on
the coast of Africa, could not fail of spoiling the climate, and immediately terrifying and embarrassing the
sailors of Buonaparte's fleet, accustomed to the mild
temperature and gentle gales of the Mediterranean,
and therefore ill qualified to struggle with this new
importation of tempests. Dr. B——s was satisfied
with the project of communicating to Buonaparte a

consumption, of the same nature with that which he formerly tried on himself, but superior in virulence, and therefore calculated to make the most rapid and fatal ravages in the hectic constitution of the Gallic Hero. The rest of the plan is quite unintelligible, excepting a hint about Sir J. S.'s intention of proceeding with his ram to the celebrated Oasis, and of bringing away, for the convenience of the Bank, the treasures contained in the temple of Jupiter Ammon.

No. XXXIV.

July 2.

ODE TO A JACOBIN.

FROM SUCKLING'S ODE TO A LOVER.

I.

Unchristian Jacobin whoever,
If of thy God thou cherish ever
One wavering thought ; if e'er his word
Has from one crime thy soul deterr'd :
    Know this,
      Thou think'st amiss ;
      And to think true,
Thou must renounce Him all, and think anew.

II.

If startled at the *Guillotine*
Trembling thou touch the dread machine ;
If, leading Sainted Louis to it,
Thy steps drew back, thy heart did rue it :
    Know this,
      Thou think'st amiss ;
      And to think true,
Must rise 'bove weak remorse, and think anew.

III.

If, callous, thou dost not mistake,
And murder for mild Mercy's sake;
And think thou followest Pity's call
When slaughter'd thousands round thee fall:
  Know this,
   Thou think'st amiss;
  And to think true,
Must conquer Prejudice, and think anew.

IV.

If when good men are to be slain,
Thou hear'st them plead, nor plead in vain,
Or, when thou answerest, if it be
With one jot of humanity:
  Know this,
   Thou think'st amiss;
  And to think true,
Must pardon leave to fools, and think anew.

V.

If when all Kings, Priests, Nobles hated,
Lie headless, thy revenge is sated,
Nor thirsts to load the reeking block
With heads from thine own murd'rous flock;
  Know this,
   Thou think'st amiss;
  And to think true,
Thou must go on in blood, and think anew.

VI.

If thus, by love of executions,
Thou prov'st thee fit for Revolutions;
Yet one atchiev'd, to *that* art true,
Nor would'st begin to change anew :
    Know this,
      Thou think'st amiss ;
     Deem, to think true,
All Constitutions bad, but those bran new.

No. XXXV.

July 9.

The following popular Song is said to be in great vogue among the Loyal Troops in the North of Ireland. The Air, and the turn of the Composition, are highly original. It is attributed (as our Correspondent informs us) to a Fifer in the Drumballyroney Volunteers.

BALLYNAHINCH.

A NEW SONG.

I.

A CERTAIN great statesman, whom all of us know,
In a certain Assembly, no long while ago,
Declar'd from this maxim he never would flinch,
" That no town was so *Loyal* as Ballynahinch."

II.

The great Statesman it seems had perus'd all their faces,
And been mightily struck with their loyal grimaces;
While each townsman had sung, like a throstle or finch,
" We are all of us *Loyal*, at Ballynahinch."

III.

The great Statesman return'd to his speeches and read-
    ings ;
And the Ballynahinchers resum'd their proceedings ;
They had most of them sworn " *We'll be true to the
    Frinch*,"*
So *Loyal* a town was this Ballynahinch !

IV.

Determin'd their landlord's fine words to make good,
They hid Pikes in his haggard, cut Staves in his wood ;
And attack'd the King's troops—the assertion to clinch,
That no town is so *Loyal* as Ballynahinch.

V.

O! had we but trusted the *Rebels'* professions,
Met their cannon with smiles, and their pikes with
    concessions :
Tho' they still took an *ell*, when we gave them an *inch*,
They would all have been *Loyal*—like Ballynahinch.

---

    * *Hibernicè pro* French.

VIRI ERUDITI,

Si vobis hocce poematium, de navali laude Britan-
niæ, paucis annis ante conscriptum, nuperrimè recen-
situm atque emendatum, forté arrideat, quærite in
proximis vestris tabulis locum quendam secretum atque securum, ubi repositum suâ sorte perfruatur.
Quod si in me hanc gratiam contuleritis, devinctus
vobis ero et astrictus beneficio.

                                    ETONENSIS.

Successu si freta brevi, fatisque secundis,
Europæ sub pace vetet requiescere gentes,
Inque dies ruat ulteriús furialibus armis
Gallia, tota instans à sedibus eruere imis
Fundamenta, quibus cultæ commercia vitæ
Firmant se subnixa ;—tuisne, Britannia, regnis
Ecquid ab hoste times ; dum te tua saxa tuentur,
Dum pelagus te vorticibus spumantibus ambit ?

   Tu medio stabilita mari, atque ingentibus undis
Cincta sedes ; nec tu angusto, Vulcania tanquam
Trinacris, interclusa sinu ; nec faucibus arctis
Septa freti brevis, impositisque coercita claustris.
Liberiora tibi spatia, et porrecta sine ullo
Limite regna patent (quanto neque maxima quondam
Carthago, aut Phænissa Tyros, ditissima tellus
Floruit imperio) confiniaque ultima mundi.

Ergone formidabis adhuc, ne se inferat olim,
Et campis impuné tuis superingruat hostis?
Usque adeone parúm est, quod laté litora cernas
Præruptis turrita jugis, protentaque longo
Circuitu, et tutos passim præbentia portus?
Præsertim australes ad aquas, Damnoniaque arva,
Aut ubi Vecta viret, secessusque insula fidos
Efficit objectu laterum; saxosave Dubris
Velivolum laté pelagus, camposque liquentes
Aeria, adversasque aspectat desuper oras.

Nec levibus sanè auguriis, aut omine nullo
Auguror hinc fore perpetuum per secula nomen:
Dum nautis tam firma tuis, tam prodiga vitæ
Pectora, inexpletâ succensa cupidine famæ,
Nec turpi flectenda metu; dum maxima quercus,
Majestate excelsa suâ, atque ingentibus umbris,
Erigitur, vasto nodosa atque aspera trunco;
Silvarum regina. Hæc formidabilis olim
Noctem inter mediam nimborum, hyemesque sonantes,
Ardua se attollit super æquora; quam neque fluctûs
Spumosi attenuat furor, aut violentia venti
Frangere, et in medio potis est disrumpere ponto.

Viribus his innixa, saloque accincta frementi,
Tu media inter bella sedes; ignara malorum,
Quæ tolerant obsessæ urbes, cúm jam hostica clausas
Fulminat ad portas acies, vallataque circúm
Castra locat, sævisque aditus circumsidet armis.

Talia sunt tibi perpetuæ fundamina famæ,
Ante alias diis cara, Britannia ! Prælia cerno
Inclyta, perpetuos testes quid maxima victrix,
Quid possis preclara tuo, maris arbitra, ponto.

Hæc inter, sanctas æternâ laude calendas
Servandas recolo, quibus illa, immane minata
Gentibus excidium, totum grassata per orbem
Ausaque jam imperiis intactum amplectier æquor,
Illa odiis lymphata, et libertate recenti
Gallia, disjectam ferali funere classem
Indoluit devicta, et non reparabile vulnus.
Tempore quo instructas vidit longo ordine puppes
Rostratâ certare acie, et concurrere ad arma,
Ætheraque impulsu tremere, Uxantisque per undas
Lugubre lumen agi, atque rubentem fulgure fumum.

Cerno triumphatas acies, quo tempore Iberûm
Disjectos fastus, lacerisque aplustria velis
Horruit Oceanus :—quali formidine Gades
Intremere, ut fractâ classem se mole moventem
Hospitium petere, et portus videre relictos!

Quid referam, nobis quæ nuper adorea risit,
Te rursûs superante, die quo decolor ibat
Sanguine Belgarum Rhenus, fluctusque minores
Volvebat, frustra indignans polluta cruore
Ostia, et Angliaco tremefactas fulmine rupes.

Cerno pias ædes procûl, et regalia quondam

Atria, cæruleis quæ preterlabitur undis
Velivolus Thamesis; materno ubi denique nautas
Excipis amplexu, virtus quoscumque virilis
Per pelagi impulerit discrimina, quælibet ausos
Pro Patriâ. Híc rude donantur, dulcique senescunt
Hospitio emeriti, placidâque quiete potiti
Vulnera præteritos jactant testantia casus.

   Macte ideó decus Oceani! macte omne per ævum
Victrix, æquoreo stabilita Britannia regno!
Litoribusque tuis ne propugnacula tantúm
Præsidio fore, nec saxi munimina credas,
Nec tantúm quæ mille acies in utrumque parantur,
Aut patriam tutari, aut non superesse cadenti;
Invictæ quantúm metuenda tonitrua Classis,
Angliacæ Classis;—quæ majestate verendâ
Ultrix, inconcussa, diú dominabitur orbi,
Hostibus invidiosa tuis, et sæpe triumphis
Nobilitata novis, pelagi Regina subacti.

No. XXXVI.

July 9.

NEW MORALITY.

FROM mental mists to purge a nation's eyes;
To animate the weak, unite the wise;
To trace the deep infection, that pervades
The crowded town, and taints the rural shades;
To mark how wide extends the mighty waste
O'er the fair realms of Science, Learning, Taste;
To drive and scatter all the brood of lies,
And chase the varying falsehood as it flies;
The long arrears of ridicule to pay,
To drag reluctant Dullness back to day;   10
Much yet remains.—To you these themes belong,
Ye favour'd sons of virtue and of song!

   Say, is the field too narrow? are the times
Barren of folly, and devoid of crimes?

   Yet, venial vices, in a milder age,
Could rouse the warmth of Pope's satiric rage:
The doating miser, and the lavish heir,
The follies, and the foibles of the fair,

Sir Job, Sir Balaam, and old Euclio's thrift,
And Sappho's diamonds with her dirty shift,   20
Blunt, Charteris, Hopkins,—meaner subjects fir'd
The keen-eyed Poet; while the Muse inspir'd
Her ardent child,—entwining, as he sate,
His laurell'd chaplet with the thorns of hate.

   But say,—indignant does the Muse retire,
Her shrine deserted, and extinct its fire?
No pious hand to feed the sacred flame,
No raptur'd soul a poet's charge to claim?

   Bethink thee, G—ff—rd; when some future age
Shall trace the promise of thy playful page;—   30
" *The hand which brush'd a swarm of fools away,
" Should rouse to grasp a more reluctant prey!"—
Think then, will pleaded indolence excuse
The tame secession of thy languid Muse?

   Ah! where is now that promise? why so long
Sleep the keen shafts of satire and of song?
Oh! come, with Taste and Virtue at thy side,
With ardent zeal inflam'd, and patriot pride;
With keen poetic glance direct the blow,
And empty all thy quiver on the foe:—   40

   * See the motto prefixed to " the Baviad," a satirical poem,
by W. Gifford, Esq. unquestionably the best of its kind, since
the days of Pope.
   ————— Nunc in ovilia
   Mox in reluctantes dracones.

No pause—no rest—till weltering on the ground
The poisonous hydra lies, and pierc'd with many a
    wound.

  Thou too!—the nameless Bard, *—whose honest
    zeal
For law, for morals, for the public weal,
Pours down impetuous on thy country's foes
The stream of verse, and many-languag'd prose;
Thou too!—though oft thy ill-advis'd dislike
The guiltless head with random censure strike,—
Though quaint allusions, vague and undefin'd,
Play faintly round the ear, but mock the mind;— 50
Through the mix'd mass yet truth and learning shine,
And manly vigour stamps the nervous line ;
And patriot warmth the generous rage inspires,
And wakes and points the desultory fires !

  Yet more remain unknown :—for who can tell
What bashful genius, in some rural cell,
As year to year, and day succeeds to day,
In joyless leisure wastes his life away?
In him the flame of early fancy shone ;
His genuine worth his old companions own ;   60
In childhood and in youth their chief confess'd,
His master's pride his pattern to the rest.
Now, far aloof retiring from the strife
Of busy talents, and of active life,

    * The Author of " the Pursuits of Literature."

As, from the loop-holes of retreat, he views
Our stage, verse, pamphlets, politics, and news,
He loaths the world,—or, with reflection sad,
Concludes it irrecoverably mad;
Of taste, of learning, morals, all bereft,
No hope, no prospect to redeem it left.   70

 Awake! for shame! or e'er thy nobler sense
Sink in the' oblivious pool of indolence!
Must wit be found alone on falsehood's side,
Unknown to truth, to virtue unallied?
Arise! nor scorn thy country's just alarms;
Wield in her cause thy long-neglected arms:
Of lofty satire pour th' indignant strain,
Leagued with her friends, and ardent to maintain
'Gainst Learning's, Virtue's, Truth's, Religion's foes,
A kingdom's safety, and the world's repose.   80

 If Vice appal thee,—if thou view with awe
Insults that brave, and crimes that 'scape the law;—
Yet may the specious bastard brood, which claim
A spurious homage under Virtue's name,
Sprung from that parent of ten thousand crimes,
The *New Philosophy* of modern times,—
Yet, these may rouse thee!—With unsparing hand,
Oh, lash the vile impostures from the land!

 First, stern Philanthropy:—not she, who dries
The orphan's tears, and wipes the widow's eyes;   90

Not she, who, sainted Charity her guide,
Of British bounty pours the annual tide :—
But *French* Philanthropy ;—whose boundless mind
Glows with the general love of all mankind ;—
Philanthropy,—beneath whose baneful sway
Each patriot passion sinks, and dies away.

   Taught in her school to imbibe thy mawkish strain,
Condorcet, filter'd through the dregs of Paine,
Each pert adept disowns a Briton's part,
And plucks the name of England from his heart. 100

   What shall a name, a word, a sound control
The' aspiring thought, and cramp the' expansive soul?
Shall one half-peopled Island's rocky round
A love, that glows for all Creation, bound?
And social charities contract the plan
Fram'd for thy Freedom, UNIVERSAL MAN?
—No— through the' extended globe his feelings run
As broad and general as the' unbounded sun!
No narrow bigot *he* ;— *his* reason'd view
Thy interests, England, ranks with thine, Peru! 110
France at our doors, *he* sees no danger nigh,
But heaves for Turkey's woes the' impartial sigh ;
A steady Patriot of the World alone,
The Friend of every Country—but his own.

   Next comes a gentler Virtue.—Ah! beware
Lest the harsh verse her shrinking softness scare.

Visit her not too roughly;—the warm sigh
Breathes on her lips ;—the tear-drop gems her eye.
Sweet Sensibility, who dwells enshrin'd
In the fine foldings of the feeling mind ;—   120
With delicate Mimosa's sense endu'd,
Who shrinks instinctive from a hand too rude ;
Or, like the *anagallis*, prescient flower,
Shuts her soft petals at the' approaching shower.

Sweet child of sickly Fancy!—her of yore
From her lov'd France Rousseau to exile bore ;
And, while midst lakes and mountains wild he ran,
Full of himself, and shunn'd the haunts of man,
Taught her o'er each lone vale and Alpine steep
To lisp the story of his wrongs, and weep ;   130
Taught her to cherish still in either eye,
Of tender tears a plentiful supply,
And pour them in the brooks that babbled by ;—
—Taught by nice scale to mete her feelings strong,
False by degrees, and exquisitely wrong ;—
—For the crush'd beetle *first*,—the widow'd dove,
And all the warbled sorrows of the grove ;—
Next for poor suff'ring *guilt* ;—and *last* of all,
For Parents, Friends, a King and Country's fall.

Mark her fair votaries, prodigal of grief,   140
With cureless pangs, and woes that mock relief,
Droop in soft sorrow o'er a faded flower ;
O'er a dead jack-ass pour the pearly shower ;—
Q

But hear, unmov'd, of *Loire*'s ensanguin'd flood,
Chok'd up with slain;—of *Lyons* drench'd in blood;
Of crimes that blot the age, the world with shame,
Foul crimes, but sicklied o'er with Freedom's name;
Altars and thrones subverted, social life
Trampled to earth,—the husband from the wife,
Parent from child, with ruthless fury torn,—   150
Of talents, honour, virtue, wit, forlorn,
In friendless exile,—of the wise and good
Staining the daily scaffold with their blood,—
Of savage cruelties, that scare the mind,
The rage of madness with hell's lusts combin'd—
Of hearts torn reeking from the mangled breast,—
They hear—and hope, that ALL IS FOR THE BEST.

   Fond hope!—but JUSTICE sanctifies the pray'r—
JUSTICE:—here, Satire, strike! 'twere sin to spare!
Not she in British Courts that takes her stand,   160
The dawdling balance dangling in her hand,
Adjusting punishments to fraud and vice,
With scrupulous quirks, and disquisition nice :—
But firm, erect, with keen reverted glance,
The' avenging angel of regenerate France,
Who visits ancient sins on modern times,
And punishes the Pope for Cæsar's crimes.*

   * The Manes of Vercengetorix are supposed to have been
very much gratified by the invasion of Italy and the plunder
of the Roman territory.   The defeat of the Burgundians is

Such is the liberal JUSTICE which presides
In these our days, and modern patriots guides;—
JUSTICE, whose blood-stain'd book one sole decree,
One statute fills—" the People shall be Free."   171
Free by what means?—by folly, madness, guilt,
By boundless rapines, blood in oceans spilt;
By confiscation, in whose sweeping toils
The poor man's pittance with the rich man's spoils,
Mix'd in one common mass, are swept away,
To glut the short-liv'd tyrant of the day:—
By laws, religion, morals, all o'erthrown:—
—Rouse then, ye sovereign people, claim your own:—
The licence that enthrals, the truth that blinds,   180
The wealth that starves you, and the pow'r that grinds.
—So JUSTICE bids.—'Twas her enlighten'd doom,
Louis, thy holy head devoted to the tomb!
'Twas JUSTICE claim'd, in that accursed hour,
The fatal forfeit of too lenient pow'r.
—Mourn for the Man we may;—but for the King,—
Freedom, oh! Freedom's such a charming thing!

to be revenged on the modern inhabitants of Switzerland.
But the Swiss were a free people, defending their liberties
against a tyrant. Moreover, they happened to be in alliance
with France at the time. No matter, Burgundy is since become a province of France, and the French have acquired a
property in all the injuries and defeats which the people of
that country may have sustained, together with a title to revenge and retaliation to be exercised in the present, or any
future centuries, as may be found most glorious and conve-
nient.

" Much may be said on both sides."—Hark ! I
    hear
A well-known voice that murmurs in my ear,—
The voice of CANDOUR.—Hail ! most solemn sage, ⎫
Thou drivelling virtue of this moral age,   191 ⎬
CANDOUR, which softens party's headlong rage. ⎭
CANDOUR,—which spares its foes ;—nor e'er descends
With bigot zeal to combat for its friends.
CANDOUR,—which loves in see-saw strain to tell
Of *acting foolishly*, but *meaning well*;
Too nice to praise by wholesale, or to blame,
Convinc'd that *all* men's *motives* are the same ;—
And finds, with keen discriminating sight,
BLACK's not *so* black ;—nor WHITE *so very* white, 200

" Fox, to be sure, was vehement and wrong :—
" But then Pitt's words, you'll own, were *rather* strong.
" Both must be blam'd, both pardon'd ;—'twas just so
" With Fox and Pitt full forty years ago ;
" So Walpole, Pulteney ;—factions in all times,
" Have had their follies, ministers their crimes."

Give me the' avow'd, the' erect, the manly foe,
Bold I can meet—perhaps may turn his blow;
But of all plagues, good heav'n, thy wrath can send,
Save, save, oh ! save me from the *Candid Friend !* 210

" Barras loves plunder,—Merlin takes a bribe,—
" What then ?—shall CANDOUR these good men pro-
    " scribe ?

" No! ere we join the loud-accusing throng,
" Prove,—not the facts,—but, that *they thought them
    wrong*.

  " Why hang O'Quigley ?—he, misguided man,
" In sober thought. his country's weal *might* plan.
" And, while his deep-wrought Treason sapp'd the
    throne,
" *Might* act from *taste in morals,* all his own."

  Peace to such Reasoners!—let them have their way;
Shut their dull eyes against the blaze of day.—   220
Priestley's a Saint, and Stone a Patriot still;
And La Fayette a Hero, if they will.

  I love the bold uncompromising mind,
Whose principles are fix'd, whose views defin'd :
Who scouts and scorns, in canting CANDOUR's spite,
All *taste in morals,* innate sense of right,
And Nature's impulse, all uncheck'd by art,
And feelings fine, that float about the heart :
Content, for good men's guidance, bad men's awe,
On moral truth to rest, and Gospel law.   230
Who owns, when Traitors feel the' avenging rod,
Just retribution, and the hand of God ;
Who hears the groans through Olmutz' roofs that
    ring,
Of him who mock'd, misled, betray'd his King—
Hears unappall'd :—though Faction's zealots preach—
Unmov'd, unsoften'd by F—tzp—tr—ck's speech.

—*That speech on which the melting Commons hung,
" While truths divine came mended from *his* tongue"—
How loving husband clings to duteous wife,—
How pure religion soothes the ills of life,—   240
How Popish ladies trust their pious fears
And naughty actions in their chaplain's ears.—
Half novel and half sermon on it flow'd;
With pious zeal THE OPPOSITION glow'd;
And as o'er each the soft infection crept,
Sigh'd as he whin'd, and as he whimper'd wept;—
E'en C—w—n dropt a sentimental tear,
And stout St. A—dr—w yelp'd a softer " Hear !"

———

O! nurse of crimes and fashions! which in vain
Our colder servile spirits would attain,   250
How do we ape thee, France! but blundering still
Disgrace the pattern by our want of skill.

* The speech of General F—tzp—tr—ck, on his motion
for an Address of the House of Commons to the Emperor
of Germany, to demand the deliverance of M. La Fayette from
the prison of Olmutz, was one of the most dainty pieces of
oratory that ever drew tears from a crowded gallery, and the
clerks at the table.   It was really quite moving to hear the
General talk of religion, conjugal fidelity, and " such branches
" of learning."   There were a few who laughed indeed, but
that was thought hard-hearted, and immoral, and irreligious,
and God knows what.   Crying was the *order of the day*.   Why
will not the OPPOSITION try these topics again ?   La Fayette
indeed (the more's the pity) is out.   But why not a motion
for a general gaol-delivery of all State Prisoners throughout
Europe ?

The borrow'd step our awkward gait reveals:
(As clumsy C—rtn—y* mars the verse he steals.)
How do we ape thee, France!—nor claim alone
Thy arts, thy tastes, thy morals for our own,
But to thy Worthies render homage due,
Their † " hair-breadth scapes" with anxious interest
   view ;
Statesmen and heroines whom this age adores,
Tho' plainer times would call them rogues and whores.

 See Louvet, patriot, pamphleteer, and sage,   261
Tempering with amorous fire his virtuous rage.
Form'd for all tasks, his various talents see,—
The luscious novel, the severe decree.
—Then mark him welt'ring in his nasty sty,
Bare his lewd transports to the public eye.
Not *his* the love in silent groves that strays,
Quits the rude world, and shuns the vulgar gaze.
In Lodoiska's full possession blest,
One craving void still aches within his breast ;—   270

 * See p. 51, in the note, for a theft more shameless, and an
application of the thing stolen more stupid, than any of those
recorded of Irish story-tellers by Joe Miller.
 † See *Récit de mes Perils*, by Louvet; *Mémoires d'un De-
tenu*, by Riouffe, &c. The avidity with which these productions were read, might, we should hope, be accounted for
upon principles of mere curiosity (as we read the Newgate
Calendar, and the history of the Buccaneers), not from any
interest in favour of a set of wretches, infinitely more detestable than all the robbers and pirates that ever existed.

Plung'd in the filth and fondness of her arms,
Not to himself alone he stints her charms;
Clasp'd in each other's foul embrace they lie,
But know no joy, unless the world stands by.
—The fool of vanity, for her alone
He lives, loves, writes, and dies but to be known.

His widow'd mourner flies to poison's aid,
Eager to join her Louvet's parted shade
In those bright realms where sainted lovers stray,—
But harsh emetics tear that hope away. *   280
—Yet hapless Louvet! where thy bones are laid,
The easy nymphs shall consecrate the shade.†
There, in the laughing morn of genial spring,
Unwedded pairs shall tender couplets sing;
Eringoes, o'er the hallow'd spot shall bloom,
And flies of Spain buzz softly round the tomb.‡

But hold, severer virtue claims the Muse—
Roland the just, with ribands in his shoes—§

---

* Every lover of modern French literature, and admirer
of modern French characters, must remember the rout which
was made about Louvet's death, and Lodoiska's poison. The
attempt at self-slaughter, and the process of the recovery, the
arsenic, and the castor oil, were served up in daily messes
from the French papers, till the public absolutely sickened.

† *Faciles Napeæ.*

‡ See Anthologia passim.

§ Such was the strictness of this Minister's principles, that
he positively refused to go to court in shoe-buckles.—See
Dumourier's Memoirs.

And Roland's spouse who paints with chaste delight
The doubtful conflict of her nuptial night;—   290
Her virgin charms what fierce attacks assail'd,
And how the rigid Minister * prevail'd.

And ah! what verse can grace thy stately mien,
Guide of the world, preferment's golden queen,
Neckar's fair daughter,—Stael the Epicene!
Bright o'er whose flaming cheek and pumple † nose
The bloom of young desire unceasing glows!
Fain would the Muse—but ah! she dares no more,
A mournful voice from lone Guyana's shore, ‡
—Sad Quatremer—the bold presumption checks,   300
Forbid to question thy ambiguous sex.

To thee, proud Barras bows;—thy charms control
Rewbell's brute rage, and Merlin's subtle soul;
Rais'd by thy hands, and fashion'd to thy will,
Thy pow'r, thy guiding influence, governs still,

* See Madame Roland's Memoirs—" *Rigide Ministre*,"
Brissot à ses Commetans.
† The "pumple" nosed attorney of Furnival's Inn.—Con-
greve's Way of the World.
‡ These lines contain the secret History of Quatremer's
deportation. He presumed in the Council of Five Hundred
to arraign Madame de Stael's conduct, and even to hint a
doubt of her sex. He was sent to Guyana. The transaction
naturally brings to one's mind the dialogue between Falstaff
and Hostess Quickly in Shakspeare's Henry IV.
Fal. Thou art neither fish nor flesh—a man cannot tell
where to have thee.
Quick. Thou art an unjust man for saying so—thou or any
man knows where to have me

Where at the blood-stain'd board expert he plies,
The lame artificer of fraud and lies;
He with the mitred head and cloven heel;—
Doom'd the coarse edge of Rewbell's jests to feel;*
To stand the playful buffet, and to hear   310
The frequent ink-stand whizzing past his ear;
While all the five Directors laugh to see
" The limping priest so deft at his new ministry."†

Last of the' ANOINTED FIVE behold, and least,
The Directorial Lama, Sovereign Priest,—
Lepaux :—whom atheists worship;—at whose nod
Bow their meek heads *the men without a God*.‡

---

* For instance, in the course of a political discussion,
Rewbell observed to the Ex-bishop—" *that his understand-*
" *ing was as crooked as his legs*"—" Vil Emigré, tu n'as pas le
" sens plus droit que les pieds"—and therewithal threw an
ink-stand at him. It whizzed along, as we have been informed, like the fragment of a rock from the hand of one of
Ossian's heroes :—but the wily apostate shrunk beneath the
table, and the weapon past over him, innocuous and guiltless
of his blood or brains.

† See Homer's description of Vulcan. First Iliad.
   Inextinguibilis vero exoriebatur risus beatis numinibus
   Ut viderunt Vulcanum per domos *ministrantem*.

‡ The men without a God—one of the new sects.—Their
religion is intended to consist in the adoration of a Great
Book, in which all the virtuous actions of the Society are to
be entered and registered. " In times of Civil Commotion
" they are to come forward, to exhort the Citizens to unani-
" mity, and to read them a chapter out of the Great Book.
" When oppressed or proscribed, they are to retire to a bu-
" rying-ground, to wrap themselves up in their great coats,
" and wait the approach of death," &c.

Ere long, perhaps, to this astonish'd Isle,
Fresh from the shores of subjugated Nile,
Shall Buonaparte's victor fleet protect   320
The genuine Theo-Philanthropic sect,—
The sect of Marat, Mirabeau, Voltaire,—
Led by their Pontiff, good La Reveillere.
—Rejoic'd our CLUBS shall greet him, and install
The holy Hunch-back in thy dome, St. Paul!
While countless votaries thronging in his train
Wave their Red Caps, and hymn this jocund strain :

   " *Couriers* and *Stars*, Sedition's Evening Host,
  " Thou *Morning Chronicle*, and *Morning Post*,
  " Whether ye make the Rights of Man your theme,
  " Your Country libel, and your God blaspheme, 331
  " Or dirt on private worth and virtue throw,
  " Still blasphemous or blackguard, praise Lepaux.

    " And ye five other wandering Bards, that move
  " In sweet accord of harmony and love,
  " C——dge and S—th—y, L—d, and L—be and Co.
  " Tune all your mystic harps to praise Lepaux !

    " Pr—tl—y and W—f—ld, humble, holy men,
  " Give praises to his name with tongue and pen !

    " Th—lw—l, and ye that lecture as ye go,   340
  " And for your pains get pelted, praise Lepaux !

    " Praise him each Jacobin, or fool, or knave,
  " And your cropp'd heads in sign of worship wave !

" All creeping creatures, venomous and low,
" Paine, W–ll–ms, G–dw–n, H–lcr–ft, praise Lepaux !

" ———— and ———— with ———— join'd,
" And every other beast after his kind.

" And thou *Leviathan !* on ocean's brim
" Hugest of living things that sleep and swim ;
" Thou in whose nose by Burke's gigantic hand   350
" The hook was fix'd to drag thee to the land,
" With ————, ————, and ————* in thy train,
" And ———— wallowing in the yeasty main†—
" Still as ye snort, and puff, and spout, and blow,
" In puffing, and in spouting, praise Lepaux !"

————————

Britain, beware ; nor let the' insidious foe,
Of force despairing, aim a deadlier blow.
Thy peace, thy strength, with devilish wiles assail,
And when her arms are vain, by arts prevail.
True, thou art rich, art powerful !—thro' thine Isle
Industrious skill, contented labour, smile ;   361
Far seas are studded with thy countless sails ;
What wind but wafts them, and what shore but hails !
True, thou art brave !—o'er all the busy land
In patriot ranks embattled myriads stand ;

————————

* The Reader is at liberty to fill up the blanks according
to his own opinion, and after the chances and changes of the
times. It would be highly unfair to hand down to posterity
as followers of *Leviathan,* the names of men who may, and
probably will soon, grow ashamed of their leader.
      † Though the *yeasty* sea
         Consume and swallow navigation up.   *Macbeth.*

Thy foes behold with impotent amaze,
And drop the lifted weapon as they gaze!

But what avails to guard each outward part,
If subtlest poison, circling at thy heart,
Spite of thy courage, of thy pow'r, and wealth,   370
Mine the sound fabric of thy vital health?

So thine own Oak, by some fair streamlet's side
Waves its broad arms, and spreads its leafy pride,
Tow'rs from the earth, and rearing to the skies
Its conscious strength, the tempest's wrath defies:
Its ample branches shield the fowls of air,
To its cool shade the panting herds repair.—
The treacherous current works its noiseless way,—
The fibres loosen, and the roots decay;
Prostrate the beauteous ruin lies; and all   380
That shar'd its shelter, perish in its fall.

O thou!—lamented Sage!—whose prescient scan
Pierc'd through foul Anarchy's gigantic plan,
Prompt to incredulous hearers to disclose
The guilt of France, and Europe's world of woes;—
Thou, on whose name each distant age shall gaze,
The mighty sea-mark of these troubled days!
O large of soul, of genius unconfin'd,
Born to delight, instruct, and mend mankind!—
Burke! in whose breast a Roman ardour glow'd; 390
Whose copious tongue with Grecian richness flow'd;
Well hast thou found (if such thy Country's doom)
A timely refuge in the sheltering tomb!

As, in far realms, where Eastern kings are laid,
In pomp of death, beneath the cypress shade,
The perfum'd lamp with unextinguish'd light
Flames thro' the vault, and cheers the gloom of night :—
So, mighty Burke! in thy sepulchral urn,
To Fancy's view, the lamp of Truth shall burn.
Thither late times shall turn their reverent eyes,   400
Led by thy light, and by thy wisdom wise.

There *are*, to whom (*their* taste such pleasures cloy)
No light thy wisdom yields, thy wit no joy.
Peace to their heavy heads, and callous hearts,
Peace—such as sloth, as ignorance imparts!—
Pleas'd may they live to plan their Country's good,
And crop with calm content their flow'ry food !

What though thy venturous spirit lov'd to urge
The labouring theme to Reason's utmost verge,
Kindling and mounting from th' enraptur'd sight ;—
Still anxious wonder watch'd thy daring flight !   411
—While vulgar minds, with mean malignant stare,
Gaz'd up, the triumph of thy fall to share !
Poor triumph ! price of that extorted praise,
Which still to daring Genius Envy pays.

Oh ! for thy playful smile,—thy potent frown,—
To' abash bold Vice, and laugh pert Folly down !
So should the Muse in Humour's happiest vein,
With verse that flow'd in metaphoric strain,
And apt allusions to the rural trade,   420
Tell of *what wood young* JACOBINS *are made* ;

How the skill'd Gardener grafts with nicest rule
The *slip* of Coxcomb, on the *stock* of Fool ;—
Forth in bright blossom bursts the tender sprig,
A thing to wonder at,* perhaps a *Whig*.—
Should tell, how wise each half-fledg'd pedant prates
Of weightiest matters, grave distinctions states—
—That rules of policy, and public good,
In Saxon times were rightly understood ;
—That Kings are proper, *may be* useful things,   430
But then some Gentlemen object to Kings ;
—That in all times the Minister's to blame ;
—That British Liberty's an empty name,
Till each fair burgh, numerically free,
Shall choose its Members by *the Rule of Three*.

So should the Muse, with verse in thunder cloth'd,
Proclaim the crimes by God and Nature loath'd.
Which—when fell poison revels in the veins—
 That poison fell, which frantic Gallia drains
From the crude fruit of Freedom's blasted tree)   440
Blots the fair records of Humanity.

To feebler nations let proud France afford
Her damning choice,—the chalice or the sword,—

---

* *i. e.* Perhaps *a Member of the* WHIG CLUB—a Society that
has presumed to monopolize to itself a title to which it never
had any claim, but from the character of those who have now
withdrawn themselves from it.—" *Perhaps*" signifies that *even*
the WHIG CLUB *sometimes* rejects a candidate, whose PRIN-
CIPLES *(risum teneatis)* it affects to disapprove.

To drink or die;—oh fraud! oh specious lie!
Delusive choice! for *if* they drink, they die.

The sword we dread not:—of ourselves secure,
Firm were our strength, our Peace and Freedom sure.
Let all the world confederate all its pow'rs,
" Be they not back'd by those that should be ours,"
High on his rock shall BRITAIN's GENIUS stand, 450
Scatter the crowded hosts, and vindicate the land.

Guard we but our own hearts: with constant view
To ancient morals, ancient manners true,
True to the manlier virtues, such as nerv'd
Our fathers' breasts, and this proud Isle preserv'd
For many a rugged age:—and scorn the while,—
Each philosophic atheist's specious guile.—
The soft seductions, the refinements nice,
Of gay morality, and easy vice:—
So shall we brave the storm;—our 'stablish'd pow'r
Thy refuge, Europe, in some happier hour.—   461
—But, French *in heart*—tho' victory crown our brow,
Low at our feet though prostrate nations bow,
Wealth gild our cities, commerce crowd our shore,—
London may shine, but England is no more.

FINIS.